# Priscilla Shirer

# one

## in a million

journey to your promised land

B&H
PUBLISHING GROUP
NASHVILLE, TENNESSEE

978-0-8054-6476-4

Published by B&H Publishing Group
Nashville, Tennessee

Dewey Decimal Classification: 248.843
Subject Heading: GOD—PROMISES \ WOMEN \ CHRISTIAN LIFE

1 2 3 4 5 6 7 8 • 14 13 12 11 10

# Contents

## Part Three: Destiny

For Mary Elaine and George
Thank you for pointing the way to the Promised Land

# Acknowledgments

Jerry, Jackson, Jerry Jr., and Jude—I love you. Thanks for letting me take care of you and write a little on the side.

To my pastor, my father, Dr. Tony Evans and the Oak Cliff Bible Fellowship Family—thank you for the sure and steady theological foundation that you've given me since I was a very little girl. Anything good God might do in my life has its roots in you.

To the B&H Publishing team. Jerry and I are so thrilled to partner with you. We can't wait to see what the Lord will do.

Lawrence Kimbrough—where have you been hiding? So glad God has caused our paths to cross—especially since I'm amazed at your perfect mix of skill in writing and passion for Christ. Thanks for sharing it with me.

To some of my partners on the journey to Canaan—Lisa, Shundria, Linda, Jill, and Rachel. We've had conversations about deep spiritual things. Thanks for listening. Because of your relationship with God, I've been challenged, stretched and . . . forever changed.

# A Note from Priscilla

I WATCHED HER. FOR DAYS. For weeks. For months that turned into years.

This woman was filled with God's power, overwhelmed with His joy and consumed with His peace. She heard God's voice on a regular basis and was seeing evidence of His presence in the regular rhythms of her life. She would pray and then believe. Expect and then see. Ask and then receive.

So I watched her. She was a wife, a mom, a daughter, a sister, a regular woman with problems and concerns just like mine, and yet her life was different in so many ways. More than anything, I wanted what she had, and I was determined to figure out how to get it. Our first conversation over two piping hot cups of tea began with a shower of questions. I just couldn't help myself. I was so curious about her relationship with God and how what she'd learned on the pew had become such a startling reality on the pavement of her life.

That first conversation led to deeper, more intriguing ones that kept me on the edge of my seat. Like a little schoolgirl with my chin in my hands, I soaked in her wisdom and reveled in the times she laid her hands on me and prayed. A refreshing friendship developed, and I was challenged to be one of the few who would refuse to trust God with an ordinary faith or settle for a complacent walk with Him. I was compelled, not just to hear about God on Sunday but to expect to experience what I'd learned about Him throughout every other day of the week. I wanted more of Him, more of His Spirit, more of His gifts, more of His fruit, more of His power, and more of His manifest presence in my life.

I must admit, it's been quite a surprising journey. But once my appetite had been whet, there was no turning back. I was ruined. Mundane Christian living would no longer suffice. Not then, not now, and by God's grace, not ever again.

I'm so thrilled that you are with me for this ride because having company makes any road trip more fun. This expedition began for me several years ago and is still in progress. God's call from mundane Christianity to a radical experience of Him has taken me down roads that, honestly, have been quite narrow. Not many travelers have chosen to take this route. It appears that not much has changed in two thousand years. While definite numbers are not known, it is believed that between two and three million Jews were freed from Egypt with the opportunity to experience the milk and honey promised by Yahweh. Yet only two of the original multitude of adult pilgrims would ever walk on Canaan's soil.

That's a startling ratio. Two in two million.

Hmmm . . .

One-in-a-million.

I guess I can see why many don't choose to go all the way with God. I've sure been in that category myself at times. It's easier to stay on the main road where there are more people and far less uncertainty. And besides, the travel isn't easy when you're headed in the direction of abundant living. While I'd like to tell you that the sun has glistened on every leg of the trip and the cool winds of ease and convenience have brushed across my face without incident, I can't. On the contrary, there have been some days when I've had to take cover from the storms that life often brings. On occasion I've had to whisper a prayer for help when loneliness knocked on my front door and came in to stay a while. When I've met other travelers willing to brave these winding roads, our eyes have met, and an instant heart connection has been made. Without having to say much, we've encouraged each other to continue.

I thought I knew where God was taking me when I first started out, but each leg of this voyage has led into territory I've never seen before. Sometimes it's exciting, and other times it's daunting. Either way, it's a ride I'd rather take with you.

I can't guarantee you much, but I can say with full confidence that you won't be bored. God's way is too unusual and mysterious for boredom even to be an option.

It's been quite a ride so far, and I don't want to encounter what's next by myself. In the pages of this book, we'll traverse spiritual territory that will cover mountain peaks and deep valleys, grassy knolls and barren sand dunes, but the journey will be worth it. With the turn of each page, you and I will round another corner. What we'll meet around one bend will bring a smile to the depths of our souls while others will create a sting of conviction that will send us straight to our knees. Either way, the prize of abundant living will make the trip well worth it. So buckle up and grab a *venti*-sized latte. You are in for the ride of your life.

Looking forward to taking the trip with you,

*Priscilla*

# Journey to the Promised Land

**Mediterranean Sea**

CANAAN

River Jordan

Jericho

▲ Mt. Neb

*The Plain of Philistia*

Kadesh-barnea

Sucooth

Etham

*Wilderness of Paran*

Nile River

Marah

Elim

Rephidim

*Wilderness of Sin*

EGYPT

▲ Mt. Sinai
(Horeb)

Red Sea

# Part One

# Deliverance

*The thief comes only to steal and kill and destroy; I came that they may have life, and have it abundantly.*

JOHN 10:10

# CHAPTER 1

# Craving Canaan

I WAS TEN YEARS OLD. I can still hear the roar of praise that resounded through our little church building that day. I remember it all—the woman standing there before us during testimony service, her Sunday suit complete with matching heels and handbag, her feathered hat bold yet tastefully exquisite, much like the others scattered across our small, traditional, African-American church.

I can still see the choir, clad in their maroon and white-trimmed robes, standing in response to her words, swaying to a soulful hymn. I can see the looks on people's faces as they clapped, others waving their hands and bursting forth in worship. The only things time has faded from my memory are the specific details of the story she was telling—some dire circumstance she had grown weary of battling in her own strength, choosing instead to obey the voice of God, then watching Him respond with a miracle beyond imagination.

But perhaps it's just as well that I can't remember all the intricate details of this church lady's story because that's not really what mattered. It was the faith she had exercised—and the God who had acted on her behalf—that even now applies to any situation, any person, any place, any time.

Any age. Even ten years old.

Oh, sure, my childhood issues were nothing compared to those this woman had faced, nor of the other adults in attendance that day with all their heavy burdens and grown-up concerns. But my issues were mine just the same. And I suddenly knew, as this woman spoke and as the congregation erupted with such joy, that my God cared about me and mine too. He wanted me to experience Him as tangibly as she had.

Almost without realizing it, I had hopped to my feet from that old familiar pew, joining the others who were clapping and rejoicing, totally in awe of the greatness of God, wishing that I could have a testimony like this woman had.

But how could I? She talked about praying for God's activity, then fully anticipating that He had heard her request and would respond to her need. I wasn't sure I trusted God with that kind of certainty.

She told of a God she'd not only read and heard about but One she'd experienced, a God she knew by sight and by firsthand evidence. I wanted that too! I wanted to see Him in the regular rhythms of my life, just the way she had described it. But I didn't really know Him like that, did I?

She said she'd clearly heard the voice of God. I never had. Not yet anyway. But as sure as I stood there, confused on the inside while praising Him on the outside, my God reached down from the heavens, dipped His finger into the depths of my being, and began to rouse in me a desire for real relationship with Him—not just for eternity but right now in time and history. I knew it in my heart. It was God, taking me by the hand and offering me an invitation to experience Him in all His abundance. He was asking me to have faith—faith like this woman had. Faith that Christianity could mean more than I'd imagined. Faith that I could actually hear His voice, partake of His power, live by His Spirit, and relate to Him the way I'd heard so many talk about Him before as I sat on that pew. That old familiar pew. That place where for ten young years I had been told who God was and what He was like.

It wasn't just talk. It was true!

And for the first time in my life, I knew it.

But over time I lost it. The ups and downs of the next twenty years took a toll on the passion I had once felt for following Christ, the craving I'd had for being a bold, bright testimony of His power and glory. Because of decisions I made and circumstances that arose, the experiential relationship with God I longed to have was too often just a dull ache in my unsteady soul. The fire in me flickered and burned dangerously dim. But the Hound of Heaven loved me too much to let it burn all the way out—just as He loves you and longs to draw you back to the place where perhaps you left Him. And in my late twenties, many years after that holy encounter on the pew, God reminded me again what He had said to me back then.

## A Better Way Forward

It was December 2004. Somehow He had entrusted me as a young woman with a ministry that was growing. And happening. And seeming to make an impact—though just how effectively I wasn't really sure. My beloved Aunt Elizabeth had given me a book to read. And, boy, did I ever read it—twice through!—all inside of the one week between Christmas and New Year's. Through the wise, skillful words of this author, God was telling me that effective ministry could never be measured by the size of an audience, by the number of books I'd written, by the acclaim of the crowds, but only by the lives being changed as the Spirit of God rested upon me. He was telling me again, "Yes, Priscilla, you can be an instrument through which others encounter Me, but only to the measure that *you* encounter Me."

With each turn of the page, God's voice grew a little louder, a little clearer, a little more inviting. He had waited so patiently through my seasons of rebellion, through periods of doubt, over mountain peaks and into deep valleys, across grassy knolls, and onto barren desert sands, continuing to draw me back to the theme He had introduced to me on that day, on that pew.

Conviction brought me to my knees. I begged Him to reveal whether or not His power and presence were truly with me as I traveled and spoke and wrote books and Bible studies. Because now it couldn't just be talk. It had to be true. Others' lives depended on it. *My* life depended on it.

It was time. I knew it.

And He was about to prove it.

That January we headed to California for our first ministry event of 2005. Still consumed with the topic of my recent conversations with God, I spoke three times over the course of the weekend to a group of around six hundred. At the end of the final session, a line began forming in front of me as many conference goers filed past to say good-bye before traveling home.

Out of my peripheral vision I noticed a woman standing there, patiently waiting for the line to clear. When it did, she walked over to me, leaned in close, and said in a low voice, "I've been delivered." Dropping her head for a second, then nervously wiping away a tear, she looked back up at me. "Priscilla, I've been in a lesbian relationship for two years. I came to this retreat with a bunch of women from my church, but they don't know about my struggle. Last night after your message, I went back to my room and cried out to the Lord. He met me in a way I can barely describe, and the desire for that relationship just left me. It's gone! I don't know what to say other than . . .

the thought of it today makes my stomach turn. God is real. I know it for sure now." She gave me a firm hug and walked away.

I was stunned and still staring behind her across the hotel ballroom when four young women walked up to me—all of them trendy twenty-somethings, bubbly and full of life—asking if they could take me to lunch before I left town. Since I did have several hours to kill, and I hadn't left the hotel grounds even once since we'd arrived, I agreed.

We took a beautiful drive through the hills of Monterey and ended up at a café overlooking a shimmering body of water. We enjoyed good food and godly conversation for a couple of hours. Then the beautiful brunette across from me at the rounded table grabbed her white linen napkin and began wiping underneath her eyes. The more she wiped, the more her tears began to fall. Another friend looked at her knowingly, then reached over to give her a reassuring pat on the shoulder. "Go ahead and tell her," she whispered.

The young woman stared down at her empty plate for a moment more, then she began to speak. "I've had an eating disorder for a long time. In fact, this is the first plate of food I've actually finished and enjoyed in twelve years. I can't believe it! Last night during the meeting, the Lord did something incredible in me, and this is the proof! I haven't had a good night's sleep in years because I always spend the first two hours of every night going over every fat gram and calorie that passed my lips through the day. But last night I slept like a baby. I can't wait to go home and tell my husband—I'm free!"

A chill raced down my spine. This is what I'd always wanted for my life and ministry. It's what I'd wanted as a little ten-year-old Christian girl, sitting on that pew in my childhood church house. While these encounters with God had blessed these women, they were also a direct answer to my prayer.

I'd asked Him as a child to let me hear Him and experience Him. I'd asked Him as a young woman to let me know that I was more than just a speaker and writer, that He was actually moving and working and penetrating the lives of other people through me. And now in the quietness of my heart at a West Coast café, He was telling me that if I'd stick with Him, I'd not only see His power at work in others but in my own life as well.

It wasn't just talk. It was true!

And here it was, sitting right in front of me.

So I've taken Him up on that offer to journey from one-size-fits-all Christian living to abundant life. And I've never looked back—except to the place where a ten-year-old girl sat in a standard church pew, wondering if God could turn a little someone like me into someone who lives like they really mean it.

He has. He does. And every time another one of His children asks Him the same thing, He does it, and does it, and does it again.

## Promised Land Living

Milk. And honey.

Jude, my little baby boy, loves his momma's milk—and he lets us know about it whenever I'm the least bit slow in getting it to him. My older boys, Jackson and Jerry Jr., enjoy a glass of warm milk at bedtime too, just to settle them down and make sleep a little less threatening to give in to.

But while milk is fine and good over breakfast cereal and is refreshingly satisfying when poured ice cold from the refrigerator, most of us don't crawl out of bed thinking about how great that first serving of milk is going to be today.

Now stand between me and my morning cup of hot tea, however, when it's been soothingly sweetened with a rich spoonful of honey . . . and somebody's liable to get hurt. Milk may be what I need, but honey is what I love.

That's why I'm glad God didn't promise the Israelites a land flowing with nothing but milk—just as I'm glad Jesus didn't stop short in

John 10:10 by merely saying, "I came that they may have life." Life is good, just like milk is good. But the life Jesus came to give is a whole lot more than good. It's not just the good life; it's the great life, the kind of life He intends for us to experience "abundantly."

Our God is indeed a God of abundance. Wherever you happen to travel in the Bible, you're never far away from some mention of His fondness for going above and beyond.

- He supplies everything we need out of His "glorious riches" (Phil. 4:19 NIV).
- He's able to brighten our hearts with "joy inexpressible and full of glory" (1 Pet. 1:8).
- The woman in Song of Solomon envisioned Him as being "altogether lovely" (Song 5:16 NIV).
- He promised to make His people "abound in prosperity" as they obeyed Him (Deut. 28:11).
- He presented even the prodigal with the "best robe" and a "fattened calf" (Luke 15:22–23).
- He has blessed us with "every spiritual blessing in the heavenly places" (Eph. 1:3).
- He has "lavished on us" the "riches of His grace" (Eph. 1:7–8).
- David could hardly come up with the words to describe His "unfailing love" (Ps. 36:7 NIV).
- His new Jerusalem is said to have gates of "pearl" and streets of "pure gold" (Rev. 21:21).

So we're not talking about a God who's thrifty in His tastes or stingy in His gifts. On the contrary, He is sitting on the edge of His seat to give us more than we can "ask or think" (Eph. 3:20). Bread and wine. Milk and honey. Life and (just when you thought you'd gotten all He had to offer) . . . *abundant* life.

Confidence—the sweet assurance that you've been anchored in right standing with God. Can you imagine it? No longer hounded by guilt and condemnation but fully alive in the afterglow of forgiven sin.

Joy—not because your trials and difficulties have necessarily let up but just because you've been graciously relieved of needing to wallow in worry or to fret incessantly over the details.

Discernment—being so saturated in the truth of His Word and with spiritual senses increasingly tuned to recognize His voice, you can be clear on His direction, even if it's not the easiest path to take.

Anticipation—an excitement that no circumstance can dull, no setback can silence, no doubt can quench. You just know that God is actively working and is up to something miraculously special, right where you live.

Power—a life filled to the overflow with supernatural evidence of God's Spirit alive and at work in you, around you, and through you.

Oh, sure, there's lots of milk in what God has to offer. Lots of depth and substance and faith-based fiber. But it's not just a life of Bible knowledge and Sunday school coffee. It's a life filled with colors and textures and unexpected opportunities. It's honey—a life enhanced with all the juicy flavors of the Promised Land—deeply satisfying but, oh, so sweet.

It reminds me a little of the Christmas brunch I enjoy each year with my mom, my sister, and all the other women in our nearby extended family. We go to the same place every Christmas season— the Zodiac—a local restaurant that's as quaint as it is classy, perfect for a festive get-together like ours. The holiday decorations are up, the china is out, the places are set with impeccable charm. But as soon as we arrive and take our seats, even as the succulent aromas from the kitchen are wafting around us, we're each served a small cup of broth. They tell us to enjoy it; it's designed to cleanse our palate. And though it does taste really good, it is *not* what I came for. If the broth is all we get, I'm leaving disappointed. Appetizers just aren't enough to keep you going, not when the main course is clearly within reach.

Too bad that so many believers have become satisfied with broth, especially when nominal Christian living and church attending are only designed to cleanse your palate for the real deal. I suspect you're as hungry as I am to get to the full banquet feast He has planned—an indulgent, delicious, abundant experience of milk-and-honey living.

If that's the "more" that's been missing from your Christian diet, I'd love to have you along on this journey. Because I'm seeking the same thing you are—an experience with the God I've spent years learning about. It's the same thing the children of Israel spent forty years waiting on because of appetites that never quite left Egypt, tastes that never could seem to get any bigger than those small cups of starter broth, eyes that kept looking back instead of looking up and looking ahead.

But not everyone kept a foot stuck in the past while trying to stretch toward a bold, new future with God. There were two—out of two million—who knew that Canaan was abounding in both property and prosperity. When everyone else was harking back to yesterday or harping on the problems of today, there were two—just two—who weren't settling for anything less than what they'd been promised.

This book is our chance to go with them. The chance to be the "one-in-a-million" who dares to believe what God has already bestowed. A chance to be among the few who dare to be dissatisfied with *status quo* Christianity. The chance to walk into an experience He intends for all His people to enjoy. The chance to be His, on His terms, but also on His pay scale.

If God has something for me that I'm in any way resisting or missing out on, I'm stopping what I'm doing, and I'm going with Him. And unless I've got my signals crossed, I think that's what you're wanting too. Let's find out together what Promised Land living is supposed to look and feel like, and together we'll discover the path it takes to get there.

Hungry? Me too.

## You and Me, Us and Him

I've got one simple goal for you and for this book: I want the pew to reach the pavement. I want the things you hear and see and believe on Sunday to be the things you hear and see and experience all week long. It can happen. It's supposed to happen. Whatever distance has built up between you and what the Bible says is true, between you and what the Spirit testifies is possible—it can be gone. It can all line up. You can live so much larger than real life routinely allows.

Trust me, I know what it's like to believe one thing and experience another—to say you serve a supernatural God and yet have no personal experiences that you can mark as being supernatural. I know how it feels when the abundance you desire is a long way from the abundance you're enjoying. But as hard as it is to say—or to admit—we've got to be honest about why it happens. And no matter what it costs to fix it, we've got to be willing to go there. To want it. To want out so we can enter in.

So if that's what you're aching for, why don't we sit down together like two friends on a church pew, taking some time to look at what this means, what it costs, and what it will look like as it happens. We've got a whole stretch of pages before us and nothing to keep us from discovering everything God wants to show us.

I've been waiting to have this time with you since I was ten years old. I think God would like us to know that our wait is over.

*It was for freedom that Christ set us free; therefore keep standing firm and do not be subject again to a yoke of slavery.*

GALATIANS 5:1

CHAPTER 2

# Fleeing Egypt

THE CIRCUS HAD ARRIVED IN town, and my little boys had come to see just one thing—the elephants. Yet somehow when the two-hour show was over, they still hadn't seen enough. That's why after we piled into the car and wheeled away from the main event area, they squealed with delight when they spotted a lone elephant feeding behind one of the circus tents. We pulled up as close as we could to this enormous creature, rolled down the windows, and gawked at the sight of such a huge animal standing so near to us, just behind a temporary fence enclosure.

Then my little three-year-old asked what we were probably all thinking: "How come that big ol' elephant doesn't tear down that fence and escape?"

Good question. A beast that big was obviously strong enough to make short work of a see-through cage like that. You'd think even a fool elephant would know that there was a lot more to be excited about on the outside than he was experiencing on the inside, going trunk-to-mouth with the same old stuff he ate meal after meal, day after day. If only he'd been aware of the incredible strength God had given him and how flimsy his barrier was by comparison—the one that was keeping him from being out in the open air, free to touch and taste, to roam and enjoy.

Jerry Jr.'s question about elephants should be asked of sheep as well. Why don't we as the people of God—with so much divine power and enablement inside—tear down the boundaries that keep us from experiencing the fullness of an abundant relationship with Him? What keeps us from breaking through to freedom?

I mean, really.

You know the feeling. You hear other people talk about how vibrant their walk with Christ is, but maybe yours is mostly a haphazard, stop-and-start, erratic experience at best. You read such powerful promises in the Word, you make one commitment after another to apply them to your life, but it always seems like you're stopping short of seeing them through to completion. What is it? Too afraid? Too risky? Too hard? Too unfamiliar? Why do you remain behind the fence line when everything you want your Christian life to be is waiting for you on the other side? What keeps you from breaking through to freedom?

Just before we pulled away from the circus tent, we found out what was keeping that elephant from breaking away to freedom. As he shifted his weight from one foot to the other, a clanking noise drew my eye down to his left ankle, where two bolts held a chain fastened to a shackle around his leg. Two bolts—that was all. On such a mammoth animal, the metal apparatus amounted to little more than an ankle bracelet. With one swift move he could have easily broken those two fasteners and walked away free.

It wasn't really the fence that was holding him in. Just a single-link chain secured by two metal bolts.

And a history of staying settled with less.

Elephants being trained for the circus, I discovered, are chained up when they're just babies. Not yet strong enough to pull free of their shackles, they eventually get tired of trying, slowly learning to adapt to a life confined by limitations. So even by the time they're well capable of snapping the tether and running away, they've grown accustomed to a world that stretches no farther than the length of their chain. After months and years of this, all it takes is a slender chain to tie them hopelessly in place—so close to freedom, yet so far away.

It's not unlike the chain that generations of Israelites were born into in Egypt, where Pharaoh, intimidated by their increasing numbers and potential power, staked them for 370 years to an ever-tightening leash of slavery. They'd become like the circus elephant—big enough in body to resist but too weak in mind and spirit to do much about it. If Moses was ever to lead them across the boundary line of Egypt or offer them any hope of entering the land of promise with God, their shackle had to be dealt with first—bolt number one, then bolt number two.

This is where our shared journey begins.

## Slaves of Sin

Israel had first entered Egypt on friendly terms when God sovereignly raised up a foreigner named Joseph to a place of key leadership in the Egyptian government. But despite the fact that they had been treated well in the beginning, nothing could change the fact that they were living in enemy territory. When "a new king arose over Egypt, who did not know Joseph" (Exod. 1:8), the chain of enslavement became a logical next step, a policy decision that was as simple to enforce as it was to calculate. After four hundred years of this oppression, whole generations of Israelites had been born into slavery, bearing no knowledge of any other way of life.

The connection between the Israelites in Egypt and our own experience today is not hard to link together. Biblical typology gives us permission to view many Old Testament events as patterns that take on ultimate meaning in the New. For instance:

- *Pharaoh* correlates to the role of Satan.
- *Egypt* is equivalent to a life in bondage to sin.
- *Moses* is a forerunner of Christ and His deliverance.
- *Canaan* represents the abundance of life in Him.

So as we look back at Israel's enslavement, we see that they were held captive by a person (Pharaoh) and a place (Egypt). Like them we were each born with a double-bolted chain that held us back from any opportunity to experience freedom and abundant living. The bolts are a *person* and a *place*. This was all we'd ever known. Life on the chain was our normal. We started out thinking this was all it could ever be, that this was what it was supposed to be like, the way it was for everyone else around us. Like the Egyptians hand-cuffed hopelessly to Egypt, like a baby elephant held by a shackle too strong for him to tear through, we came into this world hindered by a chain that was locked by two strong bolts, locked too tightly to be sprung by human willpower. The chain went by lots of different names and excuses, but we eventually learned to know it by one that, for such a little word, really packs a wallop.

Sin.

Thank God He let us know what it was, even if some people cringed to tell us about it. Fiery preachers of old were known to bellow out sermons on sin without holding back from the seriousness of the subject. But a lot of churchgoers in our age have been fed a much lighter spiritual diet. Some of our churches, ministries, and messages today stick to themes that are more likely to draw a crowd, sermons that are less likely to stir up controversy or to make people feel bad. But while we dance around the issue, uncomfortable with what the word implies, millions are left to peer through the fence, drag that old chain, and return to their flavorless fare without ever knowing the delicacies on the outside. It's simply a fact that if fullness and abundance are ever to become a human experience, it'll never happen until the shackle of sin comes off.

Some may think of the chain as simply a problem to overcome, an identity issue to resolve. The Bible, however, calls it sin and declares it an unavoidable curse. The first bolt that must be loosened on the chain is the *curse* of sin so we can be free from our captor, our true enemy, Satan. Though Adam and Eve were born into ideal conditions, enjoying perfect relationship with God and total freedom to be everything He'd created them to be, their choice to sin resulted in a chain being handed down to every single one of their descendants—to us. "Death spread to all men, because all sinned" (Rom. 5:12).

But we know that's not the end of the story.

> For if by the transgression of the one, death reigned through the one, much more those who receive the abundance of grace and of the gift of righteousness will reign in life through the One, Jesus Christ. (Rom. 5:17)

The power of sin was broken at the foot of the cross. We couldn't break it ourselves any more than the children of Israel could negotiate their own liberation pact. The only way they were getting loose from Egypt was for their deliverer to come. And the same goes for us. As Romans 5:17 says, we don't go out trying to find deliverance; we "receive" Christ's abundance of grace, His gift of righteousness, His ability to walk free from sin's enslavement. In the Old Testament, Yahweh sent Moses to usher His people into free living. And in the New, He sent His Son Jesus to offer it to us.[†]

---

[†]See Notes section on page 211.

That's bolt number one on the chain—the *curse* of sin—eternally severed in the spiritual realm, never to be reattached or hung around our neck, ever again. It's gone! It's all good! And it's all Jesus!

This is what it means to possess *positional sanctification*. Those big words basically mean that as believers we live in a *position* of being set apart, covered by God's holiness and righteousness, a secure place that nothing or no one can dislodge us from—not even us! We are eternally safe in the arms of Jesus—positionally sanctified—delivered from the *person* of Satan just as the Israelites had been legally delivered from the person of Pharaoh. Bolt number one.

So if we choose to accept Christ's gracious gift by placing faith in Him and His finished work on the cross, we can now enjoy total freedom, satisfaction, and abundance on a daily basis. Like Adam and Eve in their perfect Eden, we get the chance to experience everyday life in the ultimate Promised Land where everything is milk and honey and intimacy with our precious Lord and Savior. We feel His mighty power rushing through our veins. We never doubt His presence for one minute. We may be having to wait for heaven, but it's like heaven on earth till we get there.

Right?

## Chain of Fools

Not exactly. Turns out there's a big difference between *being* free and *living* free. The first requires our acceptance of God's gracious gift to undo the power of sin in our lives, the curse it held over us from the moment we were conceived. But the other requires an ongoing reliance on the Holy Spirit to help us live in obedience to the Lord. The *curse* of sin, the first bolt, has already been broken if you've received God's grace through faith. The *lifestyle* of sin, the second bolt, needs breaking every day. *Positional* sanctification must become *lifestyle* sanctification.

Not only do we need deliverance from a *person*; we need deliverance from a *place*. Oh, how well I know this to be true. Bolt number one was taken care of in my life when I was six years old, but what hard lessons I learned as I grappled with the second one. Freedom from a person, from the enemy, wasn't enough. I had to choose now to walk in the freedom I'd been given and to leave Egypt behind. Abundant living evaded me as long as this bolt stayed tethered.

I've included a map in the front pages of this book for you to reference as we travel along. If you were to turn there, you'd see the land of Egypt, you'd see the Promised Land of Canaan, and you'd see a great gulf of wilderness between the two. The delivering power of Almighty God had declared the Israelites legally free from Pharaoh. But if they expected to live in the freedom they'd been granted, they had to do the hard work of gathering their families, packing their belongings, loading up their animals, and getting out of town. They needed to start putting one foot in front of the other, establishing an ever-increasing distance between themselves and Egypt.

It's not enough for us just to know we're technically free. Taking God up on His invitation to abundance is how we *experience* being free. The elephant that's held by a single bolt is no better off than the one with all four legs lashed to the ground against solid steel posts. Both are equally held captive. It's not until that final bolt is broken, and kept broken every day, that freedom becomes transformed from impossible dream to daily experience. The first bolt was God's job. The second is yours (with God's help, of course).

I won't kid you. There's nothing easy about this. People who've been trained by sin, as all of us were, require some reprogramming if we're going to break out of our natural patterns and our usual ways of doing things. Living in freedom means learning how to walk again— learning how to walk *God's* way for a change—because, listen, you can be 100 percent saved and still spend the majority of your time in Egypt. Unbelievers aren't the only ones who contribute to Egypt's overcrowding.

So I don't have to tell you that there are *places* where the enemy rules, and some of them may be places where you continue to hang out. Perhaps you're involved in a relationship that's constantly calling forth compromise from your Christian convictions, but you just can't seem to leave it behind. You're still watching those same movies and television shows, week after week, still reading those books and magazines that lure your mind away from the purity of God's ideals and always leave you a little more discontented with your current conditions in life. Maybe you're bound by a particular habit that keeps barring your escape from the property lines governed by Satan.

This has been our enemy's way of doing things for a long time. Exodus 1 tells us that the Egyptians "appointed taskmasters over [the Israelites] to afflict them with hard labor," making "their lives bitter with hard labor in mortar and bricks and at all kinds of labor in the field, all their labors which they rigorously imposed on them" (vv. 11, 14). Verse 12 describes the situation by saying these task-masters "afflicted them." It's the same Hebrew word, *anah*, used in Genesis 15:13 when God predicted to Abram that this would eventually be the plight of His people. The word means more than the causing of physical pain but also "to thwart, to frustrate, to be made low, to be bowed down and made submissive."[1]

Obviously the goal of Egyptian slavery was not merely to harm their bodies and get work out of them. The intent was to destroy the spirit of the Israelite masses, minimizing all threat of resistance and backlash. Physical pain was simply the means to a desired end—the humiliation of an entire race of people, keeping them generationally subservient to the aims and whims of their captors. Pharaoh sought to separate them from all associations with Yahweh and from their history with Him, incorporating them into the Egyptian mind-set, dissuading the people of God from ever living like they knew Him. This surely caused the slave drivers to find out everything they could discover about the beaten men and women under their watch, making it their business to impose specific, tailor-made challenges on each person, intensifying the heartache by picking on every weak spot available. Slavery was no one-time decree. Never did a day go by without the constant prod of the taskmaster, demanding compliance, defying their God, drilling them in the ways and thinking of Egypt.

And this is still what we're up against today. Our enemy, our taskmaster, knows our strengths and weaknesses. He knows what it takes to keep us humbled and under his thumb, to keep us living as though we're still slaves back in Egypt—redeemed saints living "in lustful passion, like the Gentiles who do not know God" (1 Thess. 4:5). Satan is bent on burdening us hour after hour, making us seriously doubt that there is any deliverance available to us, then sapping us so completely of strength until we won't feel like calling out for help even if it exists.

I just want you to know that if you're failing to enjoy a fulfilling, enriching life with Christ on a daily basis, it's probably not from lack of trying. You've got plenty of opposition on your way to knowing joy and contentment and power in the Holy Spirit. Nobody's saying this is a piece of cake and that you ought to be ashamed.

Deliverance from bolt number two doesn't just happen. You've got to make the hard call. You've got to be radical about yielding to God's spirit so you can be free from the *places* where Satan rules. Not only do you need to do some soul-searching of your own, you need to call in the reinforcements. Turns out the Holy Spirit doesn't mind helping you find out what you need to know about yourself. Pray as David did: "Search me, O God, and know my heart; try me and know my anxious thoughts; and see if there be any hurtful way in me, and lead me in the everlasting way" (Ps. 139:23–24).

My goodness, we haven't even left Egypt yet, and this journey is already tough enough.

But make no mistake: "It was for freedom that Christ set us free." And His Word to you is to "keep standing firm and do not be subject again to a yoke of slavery" (Gal. 5:1), to "lay aside every encumbrance and *the* sin which so easily entangles us, and let us run with endurance the race that is set before us" (Heb. 12:1, italics mine).

Yes, even *the* sin—*that* sin—the one that "so easily" entangles you, the one that works the hardest to keep you separated from complete freedom in Christ, even that one needs to be "laid aside." There's no other way. There's no kind of shortcut. There's no scenario that keeps your sin and your highest spiritual hopes in the same picture frame. It takes a deliberate separation—not once or twice or every now and then, but day after day, hour after hour, time after time. Christian freedom may in many ways be a walk, but Hebrews 12 is a reminder that it's also a "run." Like, run for your life. Get out of Dodge.

Never expect freedom to happen any other way.

## Run for Your Life

So now's the time for me to be bold enough to ask, even this early in our journey, "What's holding you back from leaving Egypt?" It may be that bolt number one is still fastened. You may have never placed faith in Christ so that you can be free from the person of Satan in your life. Canaan can never be reached as long as you are still captive to the enemy.

Or maybe you've taken care of that, but there's a highly attractive sin you've just never been willing or able to part with. It may be a self-destructive habit, one that abuses and degrades your body, the same body that's now become "a temple of the Holy Spirit who is in you," a body intended to "glorify God" (1 Cor. 6:19–20).

Or it may not even be something that's overtly sinful. The New International Version's take on Hebrews 12:1 instructs us not only to eradicate the sin from our lives but also to "throw off everything that hinders." Many of the things and people that bog us down from leaving Egypt are simply "hindrances." They're distractions and time wasters. They may not lead us to do wrong, just to do less. They encourage us to stay trivial and insignificant. They're individuals who may be fun to kid around and chat with but not to charge toward Canaan with.

I called a friend of mine the other day who—like me, whatever the cost—had made up her mind to get out of Egypt and onto the road to abundant living. In order to do this, one of the things she had decided was to cut off some friendships that were slowing her progress at escaping old habits and lifestyle choices. The new announcement on her answering machine said it all: "Thanks for calling. Please leave a message. But I want you to know that I'm making some changes in my life. If I don't call you back, you may be one of the changes!"

You go, girl.

For people born in Egypt, raised in Egypt, and schooled in Egypt, the only way to taste the milk and honey is to get out of Egypt. Being positionally sanctified isn't all that God has to offer us. Secure in our standing before the Father by the removal of bolt number one, we are now free to let Him help us with bolt number two. We are able not just to *know* who we are but also to *live* who we are.

*Taste and see that the LORD is good. Oh, the joys of those who take refuge in him!*

PSALM 34:8 NLT

CHAPTER 3

# Change of Taste

FOUR HUNDRED YEARS. THAT'S A long time to plant your roots and dig your ruts. A long time to get set in your ways and grow extremely sure of your likes and dislikes. Four hundred years of anything can define who you are, even when it's a bad thing.

The brutal slavery endured by the Hebrews at the hands of the Egyptians was surely more terrible than anything we can even begin to conceive. Deuteronomy 4:20 likens the experience to an "iron furnace," with all the black-lung enjoyment of hours on end spent working in the boiling heat, pouring sweat like a pack mule, pumping their blood and toil into nothing else except the coffers of their captors.

Listen to how historian Howard Vos describes what they endured:

> They worked out in the hot Egyptian sun all day (often in temperatures over 110 degrees), driven to optimum production by their taskmasters. They had no hats to protect their heads and

wore nothing but a brief kilt of apron on their bodies. . . . [Their]
kidneys suffer because they are in the sun . . . with no clothes on.
Their hands are torn to ribbons by the cruel work. Certainly no
one stood by to give the workers a drink every few minutes. It does
not take much imagination to conclude that severe rigor imposed
on the Hebrews resulted in many of them dying of dehydration,
heat prostration, heatstroke and the like.[2]

But as we follow the Israelites through the early days of Exodus,
we see of course that they had been loosed from all that—the person
and the place. The rod and the whip were gone. The wicked taskmasters were behind them. The endless days in the mud and muck were
over. Oh sure, they might still be able to recall those scenes to mind—
in a nightmare—but at least they could no longer feel them in their
joints and muscles, in their weary backs and aching feet. They were
(dare they believe it?) . . .

Free.

Here's imagining that those first few days of freedom were the
most thrilling, exciting moments of their lives. For the first time ever,
their future held something called surprise and adventure. Instead of
the never-ending known, they were venturing out into the uncharted
unknown, following the deliverer whose God had worked such
amazing miracles to spring their unexpected release from Pharaoh.
Who knew what wonders might be around the next corner with a
Liberator like that?

But it didn't take too many "next corners" before the new had
already begun to wear off their freedom experience. Just days out of
Egypt, the excitement waned and complaining began.

I remember that feeling. Don't you? Kind of like the way you used
to feel the night before Christmas when you were a kid, compared
to the feeling you have now as an adult. My first days of diving into
the freedom and abundant living Christ was offering felt as though
a wind was continually beneath my wings, a power that could carry

me through anything. My prayer time was rich, my experiences with God real, my daily anticipation and eagerness growing. Yet over time the realities of the journey caused my enthusiasm to wane. When my encounters with Him became less potent (although no less real and consistent), my eyes shifted their focus from Him to the struggles of the journey He was taking me on.

So really we shouldn't be too hard on the Israelites for this. The thrill of living the "uncharted unknown" with Jesus is where you and I are right now, this very minute. Not knowing the wonders and opportunities that lie around the bend of any given season is something we have the privilege of enjoying ourselves, right here, right now. Today is another day breathless with spiritual anticipation if we want it to be.

So how's that going for you? Is it everything you wanted and more? Are you taking full advantage of all the blessings and abundance that life with Christ affords the liberated believer?

Or would you admit that this freedom is not as carefree as you thought it would be? Would you acknowledge that freedom in Christ contains a risky quality that sometimes makes you wish for a way of life that's a bit more steady and predictable, more familiar and controllable? Do certain comforts of sin feel more like the comforts of home than God's comforts do? Is there something—or someone—you remember from your days in Egypt that causes a feeling of nostalgia to rise up within you? Do you indulge it, or do you keep moving forward?

There comes a point when the adversary—whether Pharaoh for the Israelites or Satan for us—is no longer our worst enemy. *We are!* It's the point when, like the Hebrews, we stop looking ahead and start looking back. And start smelling something in the air that used to get us through the day.

## Fish and Garlic

College was not a good time for me, spiritually speaking. Although the Lord has graciously used much of my rebellion to teach me valuable lessons that have shaped who I am today, I readily admit that those years of mine were filled with staunch stubbornness against God. Plain and simple. Some of the activities and relationships in which I enmeshed myself repulse me to think about now. They really do. I know that some of the decisions I made, the fleshly longings I indulged, and the partnerships I pursued went directly against God's calling for my life. They resulted in a few years of painful consequences that rocked me to my core.

Yet every now and then, especially when life gets unusually hard or when I feel restless from the sameness and boredom of a particularly dull patch, the enemy tries to remind me of the so-called perks that came with my Egyptian tour package. The lack of responsibility that marked my single, college life sometimes seem a lot more exciting in hindsight than sorting the laundry and pacing the floor with a whiny baby. I can be tempted to look back with longing to a time when my life was blissfully free of responsibility, despite the fact (so easily forgotten) that it was also shot through with pain, heartbreak, and deep skid marks of disappointment.

To the children of Israel, life on the outskirts of Egypt was sort of like that. What they'd given up in exchange for freedom, of course, was everything they'd dreamed of getting away from. But when they started to realize that the open road was a daily exercise routine in trusting God to provide what they needed, it wasn't long before they lost themselves in the seafood-scented nostalgia of Egypt's dietary plan. They remembered "the fish which we used to eat free in Egypt, the cucumbers and the melons and the leeks and the onions and the garlic" (Num. 11:5). They remembered "when we sat by the pots of meat, when we ate bread to the full" (Exod. 16:3)—rations they could always count on and look forward to, even if surrounded by heaping helpings of slave labor. Maybe it wasn't as bad as they remembered. At least it beat wondering if they were going to starve to death out here by the wayside.

Let's be honest: we tend to like and remain fond of certain parts of being enslaved. We're not always totally convinced that God has a match for some of the things that made bondage feel deceptively satisfying. Unsure that He can deliver on the unknown, we too often settle for the safe and familiar. So in a sense we start to partner again with Egypt, aiding and abetting its subtle attempt to keep us enslaved, to reel us back in, to lure us away from the milk and honey, to keep us from experiencing the abundance and fullness of God. However temporary and false they may be, the bold tastes and flavors that satisfied and gratified our flesh for so long can still set our stomachs to growling. We remember them as being so enjoyable, so captivating. We slowly convince ourselves that freedom just can't seem as good as advertised without having some of these things around to snack on.

It's addictive enjoyment. Satan's specialty of the house.

What are some of the aromas from your past that have a way of wafting through your living room, enticing you right in the middle of your journey from Egypt with soft memories of what made slavery so hard to forsake?

Maybe your answers to that question will help you understand why those few fishy perks of Egypt could make the Hebrews forget all about the painful side dishes that sliced and diced their families while they were living under the unrestrained lash of their captors. Like us, they tended to forget that Pharaoh's only reason for infusing any form of enjoyment into their day was to make his slave population strong enough to be useful in building his "storage cities" (Exod. 1:11). Even now we can be sure that any good thing the enemy gives us is only to keep us well nourished enough to accomplish his objectives. The food in Egypt may have been "free," but it actually came at a very steep price.

So let's just pull the mask on this little charade. Let's give ourselves the objective discernment to get good and mad at what's been imposed upon us—this lure of eating at Pharaoh's table as though it's somehow more satisfying than what God has to offer us. Fish and garlic are no milk and honey. They never have been, and they never will be.

It's important for me to remind you that these longing look-backs that detour us from Promised Land living don't have to be sinful by definition. Cucumbers and melons and onions and garlic aren't illegal to possess. They don't come with warnings from the surgeon general (although a Tic Tac may be in order after enjoying too much of a good thing). The problem is not necessarily with desiring some sweet pleasure from the past; the problem is with wanting what the enemy offered instead of the new thing God is providing. Looking back keeps us from looking forward. That's where the true dilemma lies. The problem is in letting the satisfaction of physical appetites take priority over what God is trying to teach us about being satisfied in Him.

The desire of our heart should be the worship song of David:

> My lips will glorify You because Your faithful love is better than life. So I will praise You as long as I live; at Your name, I will lift up my hands. You satisfy me as with rich food; my mouth will praise You with joyful lips. (Ps. 63:3–5 HCSB)

What sometimes seems like less is so much more.

## Man, Oh Manna

Paula Deen. Maybe you've seen her on the Food Network. I just love her. That southern accent and down-home charm are as delectable as the food she serves up. She's an expert at combining the most pungent, exotic ingredients into gourmet dishes and entrées. All of that luscious, exorbitant variety. All of those creamy textures and steamy aromas. Even without being able to taste them myself, I can tell there's something exciting happening that doesn't ever seem to occur in my own kitchen, no matter how hard I try or how closely I follow the paperwork.

But I wonder what Mrs. Deen would do if she had nothing to work with but manna? Could she make it into something special without having butter, shortening, and bacon drippings on hand? It's doubtful.

I mean, how many ways can you dress up a bowl of cornflakes? Like Bubba's famous shrimp litany in *Forrest Gump,* I suppose a person could "barbecue it, boil it, bake it, sauté it"—make manna soufflé, manna casserole, manna stew, manna kabobs. Israelites raised on Egyptian cuisine felt just like southern chef Paula would—not sure they could be satisfied with so few real menu options.

Now let's not be so spiritually superior that we don't think we'd have gotten hung up on this too, as if we don't still file our petty complaints about the same kind of thing today. I'll confess to being a woman who likes a little variety in my fare. Having a mother who comes from South America, I've long been exposed to the spicy, gravy-laden alternatives of her native land. There are never one or two options on a plate but five or six that taste best when masterfully combined together on the fork at the same time. When I was a little girl, my young taste buds couldn't quite take it. My siblings and I would try to convince her that something she'd made was too hot for us to handle. *Her* taste buds, however, couldn't even detect the spice. It'd be my father who'd gently nudge her under the table and say, "Lois, it's really spicy, dear."

But I'm in my thirties now. I've tasted that food for a long time. And like the Hebrews being weaned on fish and garlic and leeks and onions, I now look forward to those intense, zesty flavors on my plate. What I couldn't handle as a kid is now a delight. Spice and variety go a long way with me, just as they did for the ancient Israelites.

So what do we make of this manna that was supposed to keep them satisfied for forty years in the wilderness? Were they just supposed to doctor it up and somehow imagine they were eating what they really wanted? Was their only hope to engage in some sort of mind game, tricking themselves into believing that this inferior and incessant ingredient was (repeat after me) "the best stuff on earth"?

This may not be the answer you're wanting, but it was Israel's reality, and it's ours too. In fact, it's the gospel truth: God's manna does take some getting used to. It's an acquired taste. It is solid food "for the mature, who because of practice have their senses trained to discern good and evil" (Heb. 5:14).

I'm not saying for one second that God's supply can't hold a candle to Satan's tantalizing feast. Satan is *forced* to rely on that wildly spinning mix of options. He needs all of those whipped-up concoctions to keep his plan on track, to keep us enticed and addicted to his wide menu of offerings. Only God can be so assured of the superiority of His provisions that He can present it to us in its simplest, purest form and blow us away with the difference that one tiny taste of His presence can make.

When we mistakenly think we need such a carousel of choices, we become like the spiritual gurus who parade across talk-show television, inviting their doe-eyed audiences to come to God any way they want. In essence they're saying we can let our own tastes and preferences determine our preconditions for entering into relationship with this higher power.

Listen, the simplicity and singleness that was characterized by God's daily manna was a symbol of Jesus Christ who was to come— the beautiful one-way plan for extending *to* us and establishing *for* us true abundance of life. The question is not whether a good God could possibly be so restrictive as to confine our path of redemption to one available option. The better question, after all that we've done to resist and reject Him, is why He chose to open the one path He did.

He is our "bread of life" (John 6:48). He is heaven's ultimate manna. And while the manna of the wilderness could not provide eternal life, the living "bread" (v. 50) did and will to anyone who will receive it. He is God's miraculous portion given not to bore us but to show us a little more of Himself every day. He does not become dull and tasteless by being our "narrow way." Rather, He becomes a daily expression of the unfathomable love of God, served fresh with the morning dew, the way only a caring, compassionate Father would do it.

## Surprisingly Delicious

What was apparently lost on the Hebrews is the same thing we, too, can misplace when comparing God's steady, clockwork provision with Satan's full-range food court of empty-calorie options: *the manna was awesome!* The Bible describes it in Numbers 11:7 as being "like coriander seed" (an aromatic herb native to the region) and like "bdellium" in appearance (a fragrant resin used to make perfume, which was notable from Genesis 2:12 as being present in the vicinity of the garden of Eden). The taste of manna "was like wafers with honey" (Exod. 16:31). It may have looked something like porridge, some scholars believe, but it actually tasted more like Krispy Kreme doughnuts. It was indeed the "bread of heaven" (Ps. 78:24 NKJV), the original angel food cake![3]

So *this* was the food they turned up their noses at?

Just because the sharp, strong bite of their beloved Egyptian foods had become preferred tastes of choice in their mouths did not mean that nothing else had the power to satisfy them. In fact, God likely created the moist, sweet manna to serve as a marked contrast to their monster-breath favorites, those fire-breathing flavors that had so long grown delectable to palates poisoned by Egypt's influence. The purity of God's nightly manna against the harsh, high-heat quality of onions and garlic was not merely an ongoing gift of nourishment but also the beginning of a long process to wean the Hebrews from their former loves.

It was a clear change of taste.

God seemed eager, didn't He, to get the taste and desire for sin out of their lives—just as He desires to get it out of ours—so that we can become "wise in what is good and innocent in what is evil" (Rom. 16:19). While the enemy works overtime to keep us addicted to past likes, God relentlessly shapes us through wise amounts of blessing and correction to make us want what's really good for us, till we can truly "taste and see that the LORD is good" (Ps. 34:8). He refuses to offer us anything that would excite our prior obsessions, knowing that if we are ever to start living like free men and women, we need to start eating like it.

The manna He's asked you to chew on right now may be tough to swallow, but it's the process through which your taste buds will be renovated and refined. I know it's different. It's supposed to be. Anything less, and years from now you'll still be longing for a seat at Pharaoh's table.

The young prophet Daniel serves as a fitting testimony to this. After the fall of Jerusalem, he was among the few that had been hand selected from among Israel's youths to be brought into King Nebuchadnezzar's royal court, where they could be indoctrinated in the pagan ways of Babylon. Not terribly unlike the Egyptian Pharaoh, Nebuchadnezzar was intent on getting the God of Israel off the minds of these purebred Hebrews, training them for lives of unquestioning service to the king.

The reprogramming of their young Jewish minds was a three-year process, during which time they would be taught the literature and languages of the Chaldeans, as well as being so thoroughly nourished by the food of Babylon that they would develop a taste for the signature flavors and spices of their adopted homeland. Even their names were changed to reflect their new connection with the reigning world empire. Daniel's name, for example, became Belteshazzar— the "Bel" coming from the name of a pagan God. Every time he and his companions were referred to by name, it would be another occasion for cementing their newfound allegiance to another culture.

You probably remember what happened next. "Daniel made up his mind that he would not defile himself with the king's choice food or with the wine which he drank; so he sought permission from the commander of the officials that he might not defile himself" (Dan. 1:8). But Nebuchadnezzar's advisors were certain that Daniel's refusal to partake of the king's fare would quickly reveal itself by withering his strength and physical prowess.

Yet Daniel persisted, eventually winning over his suspicious handlers by posing his theory as a test to prove the validity of his convictions. He asked that he and his three friends (the soon-to-be biblical heroes known by their Babylonian names Shadrach, Meshach, and Abednego) be served simple meals of vegetables and water, while the other young men continued to feast on the choice selections prepared in the king's kitchens.

Like always, simple purity and a determined desire for God's holiness carried the day. Daniel had been right: the tastes and textures prescribed by the Lord for the people He loves were the ones that were really best for them. God never fails to bring about abundant living in those who receive His gifts with confident gratitude. Rather than grumbling and complaining, at which the Hebrews became quite proficient (not that we haven't given their poor record a run for its money), we must accept His ways, knowing that they are designed as much for our good as they are for His glory.

## Good Eats

I don't know what equates to Egypt's fish and garlic in your own life, or to Babylon's "choice food and wine" as it relates to your physical wants and appetites. It may literally be *food*, a seemingly insatiable desire to use sweets and sodas and such as medicinal fillers for the holes in your emotional makeup. It may be the thrill of a certain sin, the spontaneity of a sexually immoral flirtation or relationship, the investment of huge chunks of time into scouring for entertainment or sports news on the Internet. It could be anything. It could be a taste you start thinking about in the day and seek to satisfy after work. But you know in your heart that even though its appeal is strong and can be temporarily filling, it eventually is exposed as being dead wrong or perhaps just a complete waste of effort. You still kind of like it, but it does leave you feeling bloated and in need of a spiritual Rolaids. Or maybe thin and still hungry, even though you just ate.

Israel had been loosed from Egypt's legal hold on them by way of Moses' deliverance. But even with their bodies positioned somewhere outside their captive's quarters, they still carried a lot of Egypt around inside them. They needed to ask themselves, just as Daniel asked himself—just as we need also to ask ourselves—Whose service do we want to be suitable for? The "father of lies" behind the pagan king? Or the "Father of lights, with whom there is no variation or shifting shadow" (James 1:17)?

Those old perks from Egypt aren't as sweet as they seem, I promise you. They'll dangle the goods, but they'll always burn you in the end. God has made provision for you to experience abundant life without having to blow your diet on things that can only succeed in making you less happy with the person you're turning out to be. Trust His provision to be complete, perfectly suited, right on time, and always sufficient. See if it's not the best thing you ever tasted, without all the bitter aftereffects.

Your manna's up. Enjoy.

*For even as the body is one and yet has many members, and all the members of the body, though they are many, are one body, so also is Christ.*

1 CORINTHIANS 12:12

CHAPTER 4

# Church Challenged

I HAD ONLY JUST MET her, but it was as though we'd known each other for years. The similarities in our backgrounds and passions were strikingly alike. We'd both been connected for decades with churches where strong Bible teachers delivered the principles of Scripture with clarity and zeal. We'd both been theologically trained in institutions of higher learning that shared the same manner of reverence for the Word. We'd both grown busy with our families while also becoming more deeply ingrained in ministry.

And we were both dying of thirst.

This, more than anything else, is what knit our hearts so quickly and earnestly as we sat together in an upstairs hotel room, gentle worship music playing in the background. God had placed in this dear sister a holy hunger for more than just a simple knowledge of Him, more than just the right answers to all the same questions.

She was desperate to experience everything God had for her, yearning for His Spirit to be fully at work, aching to know Him in ever-fresh, ever-new ways—abundant experiences the Bible assures to those who abandon themselves to belief. It's the "inheritance of those who fear Your name" (Ps. 61:5).

I could relate. I've been in a Bible-teaching, nondenominational church my entire life. My father, in fact, is the pastor. He's led this church, filled with some of the most precious believers on earth, since I was one year old, and my family and I remain an active part of it even today.

But that doesn't mean a girl can't get thirsty every now and then. The foundation had been poured extremely well and sound. Now I could sense that God wanted to build upon it a structure of experience with Him. And up in that hotel room, we two were panting for living water, tumbling to our knees in shared craving for more of God.

Those are precious, impactful moments—those times when you find someone who truly knows what you're talking about when you express your gnawing hunger to know God more intimately, to expect His power to flow, to experience the indwelling Holy Spirit in some tangible way, to anticipate His supernatural activity in the midst of everyday existence.

One reason such encounters with others are so rich and memorable is because too many times those same admissions of thirst and belief can be met on the other end by spiritual suspicion. People suddenly look for the quickest way to change the subject, to compliment your cute outfit, to tell you about the great sale on purses at JCPenney. Your honest appeal for them to join you in praying for God's Spirit to awaken your hearts can be deflected by their long list of lunch appointments that will keep you needing to wait till next week for a time to get together—if then, if ever.

God is sometimes just too big for church people. I know. Because I've been one of them.

Every church has its strengths. As I've said, ours is known for its solid biblical teaching from my father and the associate pastors, as well as its great organization of outreach programs and services. Can I be honest here and just admit that I've grown a bit spoiled? Experiencing church like this is all I've ever known since its humble beginnings some thirty years ago. I couldn't imagine God being any bigger or greater than what I'd already seen of Him in this fabulous place, where His name is mightily praised and His compassionate, redeeming love is fully on display.

Without realizing it, I had put God into a box—a box whose four sides had been defined almost exclusively by what I'd learned and experienced inside the four walls of this one particular church. From this kind of environment—healthy, foundational, and inspiring as it is—I came to the point around age thirty where complacency had encircled me like a shroud. Not in my church but in my life. And I couldn't understand why—not with such an amazing church like this to call home, a place where God had grown and developed me so faithfully for so long.

But through the years even my own father has admitted that our church—like any church—has its weaknesses, that maybe there is much to be experienced about God we haven't mastered. So it would be inappropriate and limiting for anyone to define God solely on what they've learned in one setting, and yet this is precisely what I had unknowingly done. So when the complacency settled in, and I immediately tried thinking of how to deal with this matter at "home," for the first time in my life I found myself bumping up against the sides of that box.

Suddenly part of me wasn't so sure that trying to fight this feeling was worth the risk. I didn't know what the Lord would require of me for this complacency to be removed; and, honestly, as the pastor's daughter, I felt too many eyes were pointed my direction as I tried figuring out how to tear it off and reach for new life. Others might misunderstand. People might lose respect for me. I might just end up making myself look foolish or be too uncomfortable to go where God might lead. But as God orchestrated my meeting with other believers whose views of Him were in many ways different from mine, I felt compelled to explore what they were bringing to the table.

Unfamiliar? Yes.

Unusual? Sometimes.

I was a bit nervous, but I didn't want to miss out on a shower of blessing.

## Be Careful What You Wish For

I'd pulled on my running shoes and left the house before anyone had awakened that morning. My husband and our three sons, Jackson, Jerry Jr., and Jude, were cozily tucked under their covers, unaware that morning was upon them. It was a hot, humid morning, and the sun was nowhere in sight. My upward gaze was met with dense, dark clouds that didn't give the sun an opportunity to shine. I stretched quickly and started on my normal route through the neighborhood. I enjoyed this path that led me in and out of familiar streets lined with aged trees and homes that were several decades old. The neighborhood was settled, peaceful, and mature. When I came to the back of the community, I noticed the road that had been paved to make room for new housing was now open. I decided to take this untrodden, unfamiliar path.

The trees had been torn down to make room for the cookie-cutter homes that would soon be erected in their places. The once forest-like area was bare and bland, giving me clear sight into the southern Texas sky. With no obstruction blocking my view, I could see the billowing clouds even more clearly now. The farther south I looked, the more heavy and dark they appeared. A storm was imminent.

Instead of being immediately concerned, the sight of looming thunderstorms prompted me to pray about what this sight seemed to represent to me spiritually. I asked God to allow His presence to rain in my life just as it appeared the rain would pour down on my neighborhood. My prayer was that His presence would hang low like these clouds. I begged God for spiritual rain, and as if on cue, the clouds in the darkened sky responded. They opened with shocking suddenness, and a torrent of rain pounded down to the earth. My simple T-shirt and thin running pants were no match for the droplets that fell like pellets of metal. Stunned, I stopped in my tracks, covered my head with my hands, turned around, and headed for the comfort and shelter of home. People that drove by on their way to work looked out their car windows with pitiful, sympathetic faces. They felt sorry for the poor girl stuck in the rain.

*Silly woman. What did you think would happen?*

My steady yet fairly slow pace quickened now. I was running full speed. I had to get home, back to the shelter that would shield me from downpour.

I ran.

The Spirit spoke.

*"This is what My people do, Priscilla. They pray for rain, and when it pours, they run back home."*

Yes, we want God to move. We ask Him to. We pray with boldness that the cloak of complacency will be removed, that the windows of heaven will open and He will display His glory and power to us and through us. We anxiously await His wonders in our everyday living, but when His move ends up moving *us*, we aren't too sure anymore. Running in the rain is a tad uncomfortable. When He calls us down a path we've not traveled before, around people we've not fellowshipped with before, we become concerned and cautious. This new, unfamiliar path under the rain of heaven stretches our limited view of His majesty, breaking open the narrow boundaries of our religious habits and belief systems. His Spirit quickens our own spirit to His fruit, His gifts, and His overwhelmingly abundant power available to us. We've not felt this before, and we're not sure we like it—especially when others are passing by, peering out from their own pious safe havens with sullen expressions that reveal the way they really feel about believers caught up in the surge of the unusual. It's easier to remain in the safety of where we've always been, doing the things we've always done. When the heavens open, when the wind of God's Spirit and the rain of His presence shower down upon us, we're uncomfortable beneath the torrent of the unfamiliar. And so we run for cover—back to the comfort zone that has kept us from really experiencing God as He now wants to be experienced.

I'm sure those who were passing by that day thought I'd completely lost it when I stopped just short of my house, stood underneath the pouring heavens, opened my arms wide, and turned my face upward. God's message was burning so passionately in my heart, I couldn't keep going. With His word stirring conviction within me, I prayed, "Lord, let it rain, and give me the courage to stand under the heavens when it does. Cause me to be willing to go where You take me, even if the path is unfamiliar. Tear down any man-made religious walls that may keep me from seeing You fully. Forgive me for always running back home." I knew He was preparing me for a new path. I needed to be open to receiving it.

It took a heavy dose of divine courage and spiritual openness before I could actually step out into the unknown. It took God's exposing me to a series of real miracles—experiences that rattled my spiritual cage and refused to fit neatly inside the file drawers I had carefully set up for God to reside in. I wasn't sure what He was going to do next, but I decided I simply couldn't stand to be left behind. As the name of our ministry now proclaims, it was time to start "Going Beyond."

Someone I barely knew told me about a local home Bible study where God's Spirit was on the move and where no one would be familiar with me. Frankly, I hadn't been open to committing myself to an ongoing meeting with a multi-denominational group like this before. But things were different now. The depth of my spiritual thirst and curiosity led me to supplement membership at my church with this Bible study group comprised of people who came from totally different backgrounds. Everything about this group was different: their style of worship and prayer, for one. And yet I knew from the first meeting that these people were under an open heaven. I could almost feel the raindrops on my face as I walked through the front door. I was surprised to feel such refreshment from the first meeting—refreshed by the parts that were familiar and doubly refreshed by the parts that weren't. God was so much bigger than I'd ever imagined, and it took a group of people totally different from me to help me see just how much. For one of the first times in my life, I chose to step into a spiritual river that was wider than the stream I grew up swimming in. And I've never regretted it.

Now let me stop you right here. Oh, how I wish we were sitting across from each other at the Cracker Barrel right now devouring some fresh-out-of-the-oven pancakes saturated in butter and sweet maple syrup. I'd take a break from my fork shoveling long enough to look you squarely in the eyes and tell you three important things.

First, there is good reason to be leery of what some people trail into under the guise of satisfying their spiritual hunger, even innocently so. The Bible doesn't address false gospels and false teachings so frequently just because it seemed like a good first-century suggestion, nor is discernment prized as a sought-after treasure merely once or twice in the biblical record. The risk of getting spun up in experiences that run from the wacko to the genuinely dangerous is a real concern when we start opening ourselves more fully to new things. Our age has seen a renewed blurring between orthodox Christianity and the practices of other religions that don't share our belief in biblical truth. Not all ways lead to God, and not all things that sound spiritual are edifying of the Lord Jesus or appropriate for His people. If you find yourself questioning whether something is or isn't of God, let the Bible be your guide. The Holy Spirit will never lead you in a direction that runs counter to His Word.

Second, I'm not encouraging you to abandon the church where you currently worship. I've certainly not done so. I do believe there are certain situations, in certain churches, that can become unstable enough to consider such a move, but generally speaking, running to another church that seems to suit you better at the moment tends to become a church-hopping pattern that's not good for anybody. I want you to be fully committed where the Lord has planted you. (This is where I'd stop talking, take another wonderful bite of pancakes, chew, and swallow. I'm staring at you again.)

Third, I'm not even suggesting that seeking out a new prayer partner or Bible study group from a wider spectrum of the Christian population is necessarily God's desire for you. It would be out of context with the whole point of this chapter (which is, God is always bigger than the spiritual boxes we place Him in) to declare with universal certainty that He will choose the same path for you as He's chosen for me. He may have something totally different in mind for you. But each of us needs to consider carefully whether or not we're open to learning about God through the experiences of others—others who worship differently, pray differently, and emphasize certain aspects of God that your church perhaps doesn't. I'm amazed at how much believers miss out on because we choose to amputate another part of His body.

However, if the people and atmosphere in your church are routinely stifling your spiritual hunger, if you don't feel welcome to believe God for the supernatural, if you're laughed at behind your back for taking this Christian thing a bit too seriously, or if you can't get comfortable expressing yourself because too many familiar eyes are on you, you need to get around some people every once in a while who won't inhibit you, who won't watch you too closely, and who aren't afraid to lay it all on the line for Jesus. Going beyond means becoming willing to step outside your cozy comfort zone.

## Rabble Rousers

OK, so what does all of this have to do with getting Israel delivered from Egypt? Look back to the passage in Numbers 11 where the subject of fish and onions and garlic first entered the Israelite discussion, and fix a bead on the people who started all this complaining to begin with: "the rabble who were among them" (v. 4).

Israel's interest in returning to the land of their enslavement was instigated by the "rabble" or riffraff who lived on the fringe of camp. This grouping of people was mainly a mixed multitude of nationalities who had come out of Egypt with God's people but never fully assimilated with them or took on Israel's values and standards.[4] Sure, they were relieved to be free from the heaviness of Egyptian bondage, but they hadn't really bought into the larger reasons God had sprung His people from slavery. They didn't feel the same sense of calling to follow hard after God.

Verse 4 tells us a lot. "The riff-raff among the people had a craving and soon they had the People of Israel whining, 'Why can't we have meat?'" (v. 4 *The Message*). Not only does it identify the first wave of grumblers; it also shows how discontentment began to spread through the Israelite mind-set like a forest fire, infecting nearly all of God's people with an indifference toward His goodness, a wicked ingratitude for His blessing, and a misplaced hunger for the same-old, same-old. The murmuring of the "rabble" had a contagious quality about it. This contingent of naysayers urged a continued love affair with the ways and means of Egypt or at the very least a doubtful expectation that God had much of a Promised Land worth pursuing.

Take a look around you and consider the company you keep. As you think of your closest relationships—even those who share a pew with you on Sunday mornings—do they largely consist of the "rabble," the riffraff—people who are saved, people who are freed from the enemy's hold, but who are pursuing God's fullness with only a halfhearted interest? Are they mere churchgoers, Christians in name only, people who are along for the journey but mainly just riding on the coattails of others? Make no mistake about it, their attitude will inevitably affect yours.

What would be the change in your experience if you were to seek God and ask Him to send you those men and women who are passionately pursuing His heart, people who are following wherever He leads, even at the expense of cost and comfort, even with unmapped territory lingering out there on the horizon? What would happen if you deliberately sought them out? What if your best friends were people whose presence aroused in you a pursuit for something more than what you've known to be true of God up to this point? What if your desire for having firsthand encounters with God was continually being fueled by close friends and acquaintances whose experiences with Him were a common, natural topic of conversation? How fast and freely would they keep you sprinting for the Promised Land?

## Zoning Out

"Don't let church obscure your view of God," I heard one author say.[5] Church was never intended to be a hindrance between you and the full experience of abundant living with Christ. Just the opposite, church is the blessed fellowship with God and with others that is meant to surround you with fellow travelers who are hungry for holiness, given to service, passionate in prayer, and eager to encourage. It's what they do for you; it's what you do for them; it's what honors

God the most—when we get serious together about the things that matter most to Him.

But even a church that's biblically grounded can sometimes be guilty of stripping the Word of experience and expectation. It can be filled with people who are more interested in how they look on the pew than how their lives are supposed to be impacted while they're sitting on it. Equally so, there are congregations that focus so much on emotion and experience that the Word has taken a backseat.

Jesus declared that the words spoken to His followers "are spirit and are life" (John 6:63). They are not only to be studied, examined, and meticulously cross-referenced; they are to be actively watched and engaged for evidence of God's current-event involvement, right here in our own time and space. Both of these are important and must be balanced in each of our lives. His precious Word is supposed to be heeded with authority, then to walk off our church pews and into our day by the Spirit's power. It should become what we *expect* to happen, not what we merely recognize as having happened centuries ago.

Does this kind of expectation characterize your Sunday school class? Are your worship services alive with wonder at what God wants to do next in you and in your fellowship? If someone wandered in accidentally to a committee meeting or a church-wide function, would they know they weren't at the Rotary Club? Would they see people on their knees in prayer? Would they overhear more than ball scores and weather reports? Would they know they were among people whose eyes are on Canaan, whose hearts beat to serve the living God, whose reason for being together is to be in His presence and to expect His Holy Spirit to unite them in direction and purpose?

Look, there is no perfect church. We could all find issues to point at and problems to address. This is not an invitation to keep picking on the pastor or to blame Sister So-and-So for being such a stick-in-the-mud. Yes, some in the church are responsible for shepherding the flock and leading it on mission with wisdom from God, but we are *all* responsible for how we relate to the Father. If you're displeased with what you're experiencing as a Christian, I'll admit that others may not be helping much. Still, it's not ultimately their fault. If it feels like there's a block between you and open communication with the Father, you need to be looking hard at the person who uses your toothbrush.

But do you feel like you're having to choose between church and God? Is there something more you know the Bible promises to believers that your church seems oblivious to, perhaps even opposed to?

Leslie knows how you feel. She is a young woman in her late twenties who has long been a Christian but is really just now beginning to own it, to take it seriously, to dig into the Word for herself. But as she matures spiritually, she's beginning to realize that a good number of the traditions and staunchly held beliefs she was taught at home and in her strict, legalistic denomination don't seem to coincide with Scripture. She feels bound by man-made rules she's not seeing in the Bible.

Michelle is in her fifties, also a longtime Christian and faithful to her denomination, but the things God has been doing in her life lately have just been phenomenal—simply some of the most intimate experiences she's ever had with Him before. She's never felt this close to God, this eager to meet Him in the morning, hardly able to shut it off and go to bed at night. But it's been primarily a personal thing. She really wouldn't feel too comfortable sharing how she's feeling when she prays and studies and meditates on the Word. The teaching and theology in her church seems so sure, so cut-and-dried. But the way God is pursuing her right now and responding to her worship is not cut-and-dried at all. Would her church call it error if they knew He was calling her this close?

Kyle came up in a charismatic church where believing God for the supernatural was just the way you did things. He was taught that enough faith could bust open the floodgates of heaven, raining down prosperity and blessing on anyone who truly believed. But these last few years have seemed like nothing but one trial after another. The same prayers that used to get results now feel like they're falling flat, no matter how emotional and worked up he gets. People at church tell him to keep claiming his miracle. Kyle's starting to wonder if this theology has any answer for human suffering.

Each of us carries around a box that contains our views about God. These are not necessarily incorrect views. They're simply the ones we've been compiling and gathering over time. Some of the things in our box have come from our traditions and upbringing, some from what our church teaches, some from what we've read in the Bible and experienced in life. Inside are all our beliefs and assumptions on who God is and how He operates. The problem is not that we have a box. The problem is that we have the nerve to put a lid on it. We dare to shut God into our man-made, predetermined, limited notions about His nature and His ability. So in essence, we stop expecting Him to be to us, or to do to us, anything that's "outside of the box."

God doesn't fit in boxes. He is predictable in His character, yes, but He is unpredictable in His activity. So every now and then, He comes along and turns our boxes upside down. He shakes up the contents. He disrupts the neat little piles we've made to keep Him manageable and our lives in order. He hits us with a situation that our theological box doesn't cover.

And we're forced to make a choice: do we retreat back into our cozy comfort zones and become disillusioned with God because He's not working the way we like, or do we take it as an invitation to venture out into a vulnerable spot where trusting God becomes our only sure thing, expecting to meet an aspect of His character we've not seen before?

This shaking that occurs is not intended to empty your box of everything that was in it. But as you start asking questions and searching the Scriptures, God will give you new information and perspectives—things that used to be outside the box—and build them on top of the foundation He has already established in you. Oh, perhaps a few things will need to be tossed out as error, but this is less of a sifting process than a construction project. He doesn't need to take one thing out to make room for another. This is an opportunity for God to grow bigger in your mind, to crack through the lid, to be one yes on top of another yes.

The children of Israel had pled with God for deliverance from Egypt, and when the time was right, He had done it. But even after all the mental and physical anguish they'd invested in wishing for a way out, they quickly—oh, how quickly—became resistant to what freedom required. Their early days on the way out of Egypt reveal a people who were abhorrent to change, even *good* change. They balked at challenge. They seized up at the first sight of being stretched. God wasn't staying in His box. And they weren't really sure they wanted an experiential relationship with Him if He had more in mind for their deliverance than just the simple transaction of liberation from Egypt.

All but two of them, that is.

One-in-a-million.

And while I'm not urging you to seek the nearest door out of the church you call home, I'm telling you there are "one-in-a-millions" out there you may need to get yourself around. Some of them may already be worshipping in the same place you do, praying like you are that God would lead them to someone who could offer the same kind of encouragement you seek. But this hunger may also be God's way of having you look for others in the larger body of Christ who shouldn't be excluded from your trust and friendship just because they have a slightly different take on some insignificant or nonessential matter of theology. One-in-a-millions aren't confined to one church or denomination. While they are fully committed to *their* church and denomination, they don't turn up their noses at others. They know their box has something to gain from others who love the Lord just as they do, even if they're a little different.

They realize that two people living on different sides of the same mountain can bring perspectives that the other has never fully contemplated before. One is perhaps more familiar with the rocky, granite side, able to attest to the mountain's strength and solid footing. One is perhaps more familiar with an aspect of the mountain that displays its trees and waterfalls, able to speak with firsthand experience to its softness and springs of refreshment. Neither is wrong. But neither is totally complete. And far from being threatened by other believers who look at things from a different angle or with a different emphasis, we should know that growing in our understanding of God is always a good thing. Getting a little wet in a holy downpour may feel strange, but it won't kill us.

## Wild Women

As I mentioned, one of the most gracious things the Lord has done for me lately is to strategically place individuals in my life who have been there to hold my hand and to help me on my journey into Canaan. To be honest, as I've gravitated toward these kinds of relationships both inside and outside my church, I've let some connections with other people go—the rabble, the riffraff—people who don't seem all that serious about getting out of Egypt and leaving those broken chains behind. I've become a lot more interested in being with people who have as their goal a mind-blowing, life-altering experience with the living God of the Bible. I call them "wild women"—people who pray and believe, who ask and expect, who hear me out and set me straight. Don't you think for one moment that I believe I've arrived at some advanced level of holy perfection. On the contrary, I've been guarding these relationships so zealously because I'd be so easily tempted to bail out if they weren't there to give me a hand up.

I've been stunned by the incredibly godly women I've been introduced to as I've accepted God's invitation to abundance. While I only sought them out on my knees in prayer, God miraculously caused our paths to cross in the most unbelievable of ways. From the woman I met at the hotel and the home Bible study group I still attend, to the undercover, renegade, radical believers who'd unknowingly been right under my nose all along, God has graciously allowed me to be encouraged by those who are one-in-a-million—people of faith and Holy Spirit power.

I didn't know these relationships would make such a difference, but they have. One woman, instead of telling me to stop daydreaming, prayed with me for a miracle. Another helped me wade through a unique spiritual experience without judging the outcome. Another challenged me to have faith when mine was waning. During a particular period when spiritual warfare came bursting into my life, one sister gratefully fought with spiritual weapons in prayer instead of taking me out to Starbucks to help me "cheer up." These wild women are my God-sent lifeline for this season of my journey. They refuse to let me stay on the east side of the Jordan. Helping me cross over into the land where milk and honey flow (while allowing me to help them as well) is our unified mission. And it's a wild one, let me tell you.

But you and I can never climb out onto that exhilarating ledge with God until we've accepted and applied His deliverance to our lives. Until we know release, we will never know freedom. Until we turn away from Egypt, and refuse to look back, we can never truly set our sights on Canaan. Deliverance comes first, or destiny never comes at all.

We know for a fact that the early Hebrews didn't keep their eyes peeled for the Promised Land; not for many years, not until it had cost them whole lifetimes of wasted effort and unclaimed privilege. We know they traced more circles than straight lines, too few of them willing to be the "one-in-a-million" who would courageously choose to live in what they'd been given. It was too easy to stay settled in the common crowd, too tempting to accept the rabble's opinion, too comforting to find safety in numbers.

So from their example we know that deliverance is more than a starting gun, just as it's more than a finish line. God's deliverance doesn't just dislodge us from Egypt; it's designed to fill our calendar full of daily deliverances all the way to glory.

And if it rains a little along the way, it may just mean springtime is that much closer to getting here.

# Part Two

# Development

*I press on toward the goal for the prize of the upward call of God in Christ Jesus.*

PHILIPPIANS 3:14

## CHAPTER 5

# The Long Way Home

THE 2003 FILM *SEABISCUIT* RECOUNTS the true story of a thorough-bred racehorse whose potential had been stripped bare by his original owners. Small for his champion pedigree, he had been whipped and driven mercilessly in an attempt to make him perform. By three years of age, he had become a stubborn, jittery animal with a history of failure and a sharp resistance to training. Underweight and out of racing shape, he seemed destined for nothing more than being put out to pasture. Literally.

But a new owner and trainer patiently worked him back into contention, discovering what appeared to be his secret to victory: he always did his best racing when the other horses were right up next to him, where he could get a glimpse of the challenge out of the corner of his eye, where he could see the fierceness of his competition bearing down hard to challenge him. So his jockey often made sure to position him right next to the competition until the final stretch.

In race after race, triumph after triumph, this strategy turned a "dark horse" into a consistent winner.

Finally after a long, successful career, Seabiscuit was brought back unexpectedly from injury in the spring of 1940 to run the $100,000 race at Santa Anita, one of the grandest purses in all of sports. By then he was seven years old—ancient by horse racing standards. So although he had run in this event twice before, losing by a nose both times, he was unlikely to keep pace now with the younger, stronger horses.

But there he was, chomping at the bit in the starting gate. *Aaand they're off!* Boxed in the middle of the pack as they roared around the turns, he seemed sure to fade back from the frontrunners. Yet somehow he found a seam and amazingly dashed into the lead, followed by a second horse, Kayak, who was known to be a fast closer. Kayak drew nearer. Soon they were neck and neck. Eyeball to eyeball. Gaining steam, pulling ahead. Old Seabiscuit was spurred on by the pounding, snorting view to his side. He found that extra zip in his giddyup and sprinted toward the finish to win in nearly record time.

For Seabiscuit, victory required having a challenge in sight.

And sometimes for us, achieving victory requires a bit of the same.

We've started our journey out of Egypt and are on our way to the Promised Land—*delivered!* We've slipped the confines of slavery and stepped out onto free soil. We've broken into a comfortable jog, not really wanting to push ourselves at too taxing of a pace. But as we'll come to see—both in the Hebrews' lives as well as our own—deliverance doesn't lead directly to the easy life. The next stop is not Shangri-La. We're about to enter a *development* phase that is every bit as crucial to our experience of abundant living as our initial deliverance was. Freedom on its own is not enough to get us to the land of promise and make us into the people God wants us to be. And make no mistake about it, His goal is to *make us over* even more than it is to *take us over* to Canaan. If we're to know what victory feels like, not just what it looks like, we need His help in ways we'd never think to ask. Unexpected ways. Sometimes even hard ways.

So perhaps like Seabiscuit, as you look to either side, you see challenges in your life you'd just as soon not be encountering out here. Maybe you're dealing with a physical condition that's potentially frightening if not just daily frustrating. Maybe you're battling some relationship issues that are keeping things stirred up and incessantly unresolved. Maybe you've been slammed by a sudden, life-altering circumstance or tragedy that's affected you in deep, profound ways you don't think you'll ever understand. Or maybe you're just traveling through a season of life that isn't agreeing with you.

You can't imagine this is what God had in mind for you when He brought you out of Egypt. In fact, it's pretty much what you've been praying *against*. No way could He have thrust you into this kind of situation unless you're being punished for some reason. I mean, doesn't He know you do your best running without all these obstacles in your way, without being constantly hounded by one problem after another? Seems like there should be a more direct route to abundant living. This one's awfully cluttered and confusing, eyeball to eyeball with all this stuff.

Then again, maybe He knows, like Seabiscuit's trainers knew, that challenges bring out the potential in you—potential you never knew was there. It's not enough for you to be out of Egypt. God wants Egypt to be worked out of you.

Which often leads to some interesting . . . *developments*.

## Taking a Turn

When the Hebrews emerged from Egyptian bondage, the distance between themselves and southern Canaan was about 150 miles. Moving at a comfortable clip, accounting for all the variables involved in transporting that many people over that kind of terrain, historians suggest they could have made the trip in a little less than a month. Easy. Whether they were aware of this or not, we have no way of knowing. But most likely they did. With one hike up the main road along the Mediterranean Sea, they could not only reach Canaan in thirty days; they could have a nice scenic view the whole time. They had prepared themselves both mentally and physically for a fairly brief journey.

But at the intersection of eastern Egypt and Exodus 13, things started to go south on them.

Exodus 13 opens a spiritual can of worms we're still trying to wiggle away from today. With the Promised Land a proverbial hop, skip, and a jump away, God did something that must have seemed as cruel as it was incredible. See if you can spot it:

> Now when Pharaoh had let the people go, God did not lead them
> by the way of the land of the Philistines, even though it was near;
> for God said, "The people might change their minds when they
> see war, and return to Egypt." Hence God led the people around
> by the way of the wilderness to the Red Sea; and the sons of Israel
> went up in martial array from the land of Egypt. (vv. 17–18)

Apparently, God didn't have his Google Earth turned on.

But you can be sure He had the Hebrews in sight. And He knew if His people were to receive the fullness of this milk-and-honey experience, they needed to have a few things in their sight as well—things they'd never have gone out looking for on their own but things that convince a Canaan traveler *abundant* life can happen in *real* life. God wanted them eye to eye with some heavyweight challenges so they could learn how to apply His power in any situation. What good are freed children of God who want to go back to Egypt "in their hearts" (Acts 7:39)?

So welcome to the wilderness.

And don't be surprised if God "led" you here.

I'll admit, now, this makes me want to ask you out to Cracker Barrel again to talk this over face-to-face because I know what it's like to read these unexpected words of Scripture cold. If we were there, I'd reach across and pat you on the shoulder as the reality of this part of the journey sinks in. The wilderness is a place I've been before, my friend, just as you have. It may be a place you're living in right now. If so, you'd probably look me in the eye and tell me you're just frustrated with it, plain and simple.

Our wilderness seasons are probably more varied than we can imagine. You may be caring for aging parents whose constant needs and often unreasonable demands are putting a strain on everything from paying your bills to simple things like keeping up with your reading glasses. Maybe you're a single person who never saw your journey happening without a spouse, but time is spinning past and no one's come along yet. Maybe you've been married for a good while, but you've not been able to have children, try as you might.

Your wilderness may be financial—a monthly race between you, the mailbox, and your checkbook balance. It could be a career track that feels more stalled than ever, or maybe a series of car and home repairs that won't seem to let up, or a ministry you're absolutely sure God has called you to but, for whatever reason, He doesn't seem eager to get it off the ground or anywhere near what you envisioned. Maybe your current and lingering wilderness involves a tragic situation that has caught you off guard at a moment's notice, pulling the rug out from under your feet as well as your heart.

Frustrating. Plain ol' frustrating.

Or as the Israelites must have thought, gazing off into a wilderness that stretched for miles before them in the opposite direction of Canaan—dry and dusty.

## Dead Ahead

They set out from Succoth and camped in Etham on the edge of
the wilderness." (Exod. 13:20)

There it was. The wilderness. Settled at Etham, they could see
it—coughing and swirling in the hot desert wind. The last place their
tired feet wanted to take them. The wild, time-wasting wilderness.

We know from verses 21–22 that God had already been "going
before them in a pillar of cloud by day . . . and in a pillar of fire by
night," a manifestation of His presence He did not take away from
them for one minute. This was their guidance system. This was the
way they determined their travel plans. For the last little while, His
hovering cloud had held stationary over Etham, the place where God
wanted them to camp out and catch their breath. From this settled
location they could look north and see the easiest, most convenient
route to Canaan, perhaps actively populated here and there with
traders who were traveling one of the region's major roads or high-
ways. But they could also sit and look to the south, where they saw
nothing but wilderness—dry, dusty wilderness—and God's pillar of
cloud, beckoning them to follow Him into the bleakness.

What do you do in a situation like that? How will you respond
when you're at Etham with a clear view of a more comfortable route
but also a sure certainty that God's presence is leading you another
way? The Israelites had that kind of decision to make: should they
turn back and take what seemed to be the most simple path to where
they were headed, or should they continue pursuing God, knowing
full well that the direction He was going would lead them on a more
difficult route?

Maybe you're at a place like that, camped out at your own personal Etham. Do you stay in this tough marriage? Do you keep trying to parent these difficult children? Do you accept singleness as a
way of life, at least for now? Do you suffer in some way or another

without letting it turn into bitterness, without letting it veer you off the path God knows you need to take to experience fullness of life with Him?

Two years into our marriage, Jerry and I sat and stared hard into the wilderness. An early morning pregnancy test had revealed a surprise we weren't anticipating. I was carrying our first baby. And though caught a bit off guard, we were both more excited than we knew how to express. Only one thing stood between us and a real celebration: we were due to be in Chicago the next day for me to speak to a large gathering of women at a local church. We'd have to wait a few days before we could get back home and really imagine the possibilities.

We left town and arrived at our location. The time rolled around for the meeting to begin. Shortly before stepping out on the platform, I swung by the restroom. Suddenly and without any warning, I discovered that something was terribly wrong. I called for Jerry, who rushed in to see what had happened. We looked at each other in fear and panic, not sure what to do or exactly what this meant. A few emotional moments later, a gentle knock interrupted our secret despair. Several hundred women were waiting for me, practically in the next room. I had to get out there if I possibly could.

So I did. And somehow I made it through. For the next hour I kept my mouth moving while my mind spun cartwheels of worry.

As soon as I could get away, we phoned the doctor back in Dallas and set up an appointment for the following day. The ultrasound revealed what we dreaded most. Our first child had miscarried. In the space of a few dozen hours, we had gone from elation to devastation. To the wilderness.

It was dry.

It was dusty.

The sun beat down hard and made us want to quit. Nothing tasted good. Nothing felt right. But one thing was for sure: we were eye to eye with an eye-opening challenge. Were we going to backtrack into whatever shell of safety we thought would keep us from ever hurting this way again? Or would we let the foul, snarling breath of tragedy motivate us to race even harder into the arms of God, trusting Him to know the best way to take us where we most wanted to be—even if the best way (for reasons we may never know for sure) meant going this way?

Let me make something clear at this point: *the wilderness is not a necessity to reaching spiritual abundance.* It's no automatic given that you'll spend a considerable portion of your life there. Yes, we live in a fallen world, and the wilderness will likely be a part of everyone's experience at one time or another. But that's not to say with airtight assurance that some devastating tragedy is in your future. Listen, "God is love" first and foremost (1 John 4:16), and "the Lord is righteous in all His ways and *kind* in all His deeds" (Ps. 145:17, italics mine). No, He's not above using the wilderness when He knows we need it, when it's part of His purpose for how He desires to grow us and use us. But He's not One to sling us into tight situations just for fun. Nor is it just a matter of time before our number comes up.

Bottom line, you needn't be terrified of God, always wondering when or how He's going to allow a season of trouble. Neither, on the other hand, should you be terrified of tragedy, as though you could never endure it. Yet each of us does need to consider how we'll respond if we indeed discover that a wilderness experience—for us, for now—has become His will.

## Seeing Is Believing

Often our first reaction to a turn of events like this is to look and see what we've done to cause it. And granted, God is faithful enough to know—as we know with our own children—that the short-term pain of correction is worth the long-term prize of character. But generally speaking, the Bible seems to say that the wilderness is not a one-to-one reaction to some specific thing we've done. It's not typically the spiritual equivalent to a spanking. The wilderness, strange as it may seem, is often just (listen closely now)—it is often God's will. It's His chosen plan for us.

Can you believe that? *Will* you believe that?

Friend, I can't explain it, but I can tell you from experience and from the Word of God that the road He chooses (yes, *chooses*) to lead us on as we travel into a life of abundance is often more challenging, more tedious, more lonely, more indirect, and more costly than we ever expected. Not always, but often.

The historical account of Job certainly bears this out in dramatic detail. The first verse of the first chapter clearly points out that this was a man who was "blameless, upright, fearing God and turning away from evil." Everybody who knew Job would tell you that he was the dictionary definition of righteousness. He had a wife who loved him. Had a big houseful of kids. Had all kinds of property and possessions and stuff. He sat comfortably within the "hedge" God had provided to protect everything he owned from decay, ruin, and destruction (1:10). Job had it going on! And seemed to be the one-in-a-million kind of guy who could have all of that and not let it go to his head.

Then, as we know, God allowed the enemy to run rampant through Job's life—not because Satan had outsmarted or strong-armed the Lord. No, God had pointed Job out: "Have you considered My servant Job? For there is no one like him on the earth, a blameless and upright man, fearing God and turning away from evil" (1:8). Well, you know what happened next. In rapid succession his servants were put to death, his livestock either stolen by bandits or struck dead in a storm, even all ten of his children killed in a common tragedy. Soon his physical health had taken such a beating, the friends who came around to survey the damage didn't even recognize who he was.

This was a man who loved God, a man whose initial reaction to this horrific turn of events went something like this: he "arose and tore his robe and shaved his head, and he fell to the ground and"—what?—he "worshiped" (1:20). Why would God lead a person like this to the wilderness?

Maybe the answer we're seeking comes at the end of Job's ordeal. After a long, torturous run through some of the driest, dustiest conditions ever known to man, Job was able to articulate something he could never have put into these kinds of words before. He said to the Lord, "I have heard of You by the hearing of the ear"—back when I was safe and secure in my happy, unhurried world—"but now my eye sees You" (42:5). Now I know You by *experience*.

Think back to what God gave as His reasoning for leading the people away from the overland route to Canaan even though it was "near"—"The people might change their minds" (Exod. 13:17). This phrase "change their minds" comes from a Hebrew root word that means "to have regrets or a change of heart, to turn from a former attitude."[6] Yes, a northern march would have been the shortest way there, but that doesn't mean it would have been the best way to accomplish God's purposes for them. His main purpose was not to get them to Canaan as quickly as possible. He was after their minds. He was leading a whole race of people to a point where they could have a unified purpose, having God as their aim. His main goal for delivering His people was what He had repeatedly told Moses to say to Pharaoh: "Let My people go, that they may serve Me" (Exod. 8:1). He wanted them to "know that I am the LORD your God, who brought you out from under the burdens of the Egyptians" (Exod. 6:7). He wanted them to know—to *know*—that He would be faithful to bring them to the land He had sworn "to give to Abraham, Isaac, and Jacob" (v. 8). He wanted His people to know Him . . . by experience.

Deliverance from Pharaoh was designed to set the people's hearts on serving and worshipping the God of their fathers. The wilderness phase was the stage of development designed to cement their hearts in total trust and confidence in His ability to provide for them. It wasn't enough that they'd heard all those stories about Him; it was time for them to know the Storyteller for themselves. It was time for the stories to be about them for a change.

## Let It Happen

Are you in a wilderness season right now? Perhaps you're reeling from some tragic circumstance that seems to make no sense to you. Or perhaps you're just in a particular season or phase of life that, for whatever reason, you're really not that happy about. It's just kind of annoying, tiring, slow. Would you consider for a moment that this is not a punishment, an accident, or a bit of negligence on the part of God, who apparently doesn't really care whether you live or die or whatever happens to you?

Would you ask yourself what you're really wanting in life? Is it just to be happy, at peace, at ease? Is it to be left alone to do what you do without having to live eye to eye with challenges, difficulties, and shortages? Or is it to be in intimate relationship with a Father whose purpose in drawing you is to give you the opportunity to know—really *know*—this One who made you, wants you, loves you?

The psalmist Asaph admitted to getting pretty fed up with being in the wilderness. Not just being in the wilderness, but at the same time having to watch people who didn't even think about God, didn't care about God, didn't have anything but disinterest in God— watching them seem to scoot along just fine without having to deal with the wilderness. What's up with that? "Surely in vain I have kept my heart pure and washed my hands in innocence; for I have been stricken all day long and chastened every morning" (Ps. 73:13–14). And I'm sick and tired of it!

That's honestly the way he felt until he "came into the sanctuary of God" (v. 17) . . . until he drew close to the One who had been using the pressure of problems not to bury him but to beckon him. And in that place of nearness and fellowship, he discovered that being actively pursued by God was far more precious than merely having his problems alleviated by God.

> Whom have I in heaven but You? And besides You, I desire nothing on earth. My flesh and my heart may fail, but God is the strength of my heart and my portion forever. For, behold, those who are far from You will perish; You have destroyed all those who are unfaithful to You. But as for me, the nearness of God is my good; I have made the Lord God my refuge, that I may tell of all Your works. (vv. 25–28)

It's awfully easy to get disillusioned with God out here in the wilderness. It's easy to think He's forgotten you, doesn't care about you, doesn't love you. It's easy to start asking why your best isn't good enough to earn you at least a little bit of relief from this constant upset and turmoil, from the choking dryness and dustiness.

But listen, you don't have to figure out the wilderness. You don't have to fix the wilderness. You don't have to be able to explain to your church friends why you're going through the wilderness. Your job as a much loved, highly treasured child of God is simply to *yield* to the wilderness because it's often only in the wilderness where our runaway desires can finally be boiled down to this: "One thing I have asked from the Lord, that I shall seek: that I may dwell in the house of the Lord all the days of my life, to behold the beauty of the Lord and to meditate in His temple" (Ps. 27:4).

The wilderness is God's way of making us want the only thing that's really worth having.

The wilderness, my friend, is worth it.

*He put you through hard times. He made you go hungry. Then*
*he fed you with manna, something neither you nor your parents*
*knew anything about, so you would learn that men and women*
*don't live by bread only; we live by every word that comes from*
*God's mouth.*

DEUTERONOMY 8:3 THE MESSAGE

## CHAPTER 6

# Why Me?

ELIZABETH: "MY MARRIAGE HAS JUST become a total mess. My husband not only admitted to having an affair; now he tells me he has no intention of breaking it off. I can't believe it! This is not the way things were supposed to turn out for me, for us. We've been married twenty-eight years. We have four children. You could never have told me I'd be walking a road like this today."

*Why me?*

Meagan: "I want a baby more than anything. When I'm around mothers, I get so jealous, I want to cry. Sometimes I *do* cry. I excuse myself, slip away to the bathroom, and the tears just come pouring down my face. I've got so much—I'm aware of that—yet I feel so empty. And the doctors tell us there's no hope."

*Why me?*

Steve: "Why they gave me a pink slip, I'll never fully understand. I was a valuable commodity to that company! I know it. Always did a good job. Always got glowing reports. Now here I sit with no prospects, nothing to hold out much hope for. I've gone a whole year without work. Absolutely nothing is available right now. I don't know how much longer I can take this—feeling so inadequate as a husband and father . . . as a person."

*Why me?*

Pamela: "It's been nine years and I'm still struggling. I thought for sure when I started this ministry, it'd be flourishing by this time. A few initial years of struggle are to be anticipated but I'm tired of things still being so difficult. Everything from raising money to signing up volunteers has been complicated. Others seem to be doing so well and receiving more opportunities to make an impact. Why does my journey have to be so rough?"

*Why me?*

Ashleigh: "I'm still single. My thirties were supposed to be the years I spent as a wife and mother, raising a family. And yet I'm still alone. I can't believe this is my life. I'm bored and lonely. The grass sure looks greener on the other side."

*Why me?*

Two weeks after a friend of mine named Jenny placed her faith in Christ, God allowed her to conceive her first son. She and her husband, Nathan, already had two lovely daughters, so this development promised to be a new experience for everybody. They were all so excited.

Little Hosea was several weeks overdue when he finally arrived. But as with Jenny's baby girls before, the connection upon meeting his eyes in the delivery room was instant. That was April 9 at 1:00 in the morning. Now there were five. One big, happy family.

But less than a month later, May 6 at 6:30 in the evening, Jenny was busy preparing dinner when her "mother sense" told her something wasn't right. Hosea was about a half hour late for his usual feeding. He should be getting fussy by now. Why wasn't he? Jenny dropped her knife on the counter and hurried into the bedroom where Hosea was sleeping—only he wasn't just sleeping. As she reached into his crib, she found him cold and blue.

The next moments whizzed by in a blur. The 9-1-1 call. Frantic attempts to perform infant CPR the best they knew how. The ambulance arriving. Their daughters terrified. The mad dash to the emergency room. In one of those moments you hear about, you read about, but never want to know about, the white-coated doctor opened the door to the room where Nathan and Jenny were waiting, a serious, sympathetic tone in his voice, and said, "There's just nothing more we can do. I'm so sorry." She wrote the following words in a letter to me: "Is this the wilderness that God would want me to bear?"

*Why me?*

All of these stories and sentiments expressed to me through my short years in ministry beg the same question, longing for some kind of soothing response. Each of these people wonder about the biblical reality that the wilderness is often God's will. What a hard teaching to swallow! It makes God out to be so cruel and uncaring, allowing pain by deliberate decree, as if life weren't hard enough already without adding any more trouble to it. This wilderness doctrine is all plaids and stripes in a world that's supposed to match a lot better than that.

Christian faith, we know, tells us there is meaning in this:

Consider it all joy, my brethren, when you encounter various trials, knowing that the testing of your faith produces endurance. And let endurance have its perfect result, so that you may be perfect and complete, lacking in nothing. (James 1:2–4)

In this you greatly rejoice, even though now for a little while, if necessary, you have been distressed by various trials, so that the proof of your faith, being more precious than gold which is perishable, even though tested by fire, may be found to result in praise and glory and honor at the revelation of Jesus Christ. (1 Pet. 1:6–7)

These are truths we can accept with our minds. We're able to believe them in theory. But when the wilderness is blowing dry and dusty, when the "various trials" come with names and faces and find the way to our mailing address, simple belief doesn't always feel like enough to live on. It's hard for us not to turn our gaze toward the heavens and wonder aloud to God, "Why me?"

Frankly, I don't think God minds our asking that. Job responded to his multitude of inexplicable problems, "Why do You hide Your face and consider me Your enemy?" (Job 13:24). The prophet Habakkuk cried out to God from what appeared to be never-ending exile with his countrymen, "Why do You look with favor on those who deal treacherously? Why are You silent when the wicked swallow up those more righteous than they?" (Hab. 1:13). Jeremiah tried reconciling what he knew about God with what he was seeing in practice, crying out, "You, O LORD, rule forever; Your throne is from generation to generation. Why do You forget us forever? Why do You forsake us so long?" (Lam. 5:19–20).

Why?

Why me?

## Why the Wilderness?

Obviously this is a question too complex to gloss over with pat answers. Some of the explanations, in fact, are closeted away in the mind of God, reasons He knows we're not mature enough to handle apparently; a measure of understanding we won't be able to ascertain until we sit at His feet—that is, if anything but worship even matters to us any more once we get there.

We began seeing some glimmers of answers in the last chapter, learning from the way Job responded to his suffering, when he said, "I have heard of You by the hearing of the ear; but now my eye sees You" (Job 42:5). Much of the book of Exodus as well, from the Red Sea to Sinai and beyond, is taken up with God putting His people in situations where they could know Him by experience, where they could witness the range of His power in the context of His faithfulness. Part of the reason the wilderness makes spiritual sense is because it enables us to know Him more intimately than we would if left to our own desires and devices. In an unusual, unexpected, even unwanted fashion, the wilderness is God's way of doing us a favor we don't even know we need.

But that's certainly not all there is to it. If it troubles you to think of God allowing you to travel through a rough patch just so you can know Him better—if that sounds incredibly heavy-handed, borderline heartless—consider that the wilderness is often safer than the alternative.

For the Hebrews the auxiliary option to the wilderness was "the way of the land of the Philistines" (Exod. 13:17), which was not exactly a stroll down Easy Street. The plains of Philistia were teeming with hostile enemies who had no qualms with scratching their itchy trigger fingers. Not only that, northern Sinai—another region bypassed by the Israelites' route into the wilderness—was a heavily militarized zone in those days. The Egyptian army maintained a strong presence there, protected by a series of fortresses that gave them the drop on anyone marching through unprepared and underarmed.[7] God knew that these areas were crawling with dangerous, murderous opposition. And though the wilderness was certainly no Disney World, it's not as though the road through Philistia was a pleasure cruise. God was using the wilderness way to protect them, whether His people knew it or not.

Isn't that how it often is? All we know for sure is what we see in our own situation. From that grass-is-greener vantage point, it's easy to dress up our imaginary fantasy lands in colors to match the rainbow. But we can't know, as God does, the harsh realities we'd have faced in places we've never been. So in order to shelter us from danger, He sometimes hedges us inside areas that, although perhaps extremely uncomfortable and unwanted, are much safer than we realize, much less painful than what we *could* be experiencing.

For not only is He protecting us from dangerous outsiders and situations, but He's also protecting us from ourselves. Take a look, for example, at the Hebrews marching out of Egypt, assembling themselves "in martial array" (Exod. 13:18), as though they really knew what they were doing. The root word is a derivative of the Hebrew word *khamesh*, which means "five." God's people left in an official formation composed of five divisions: a forward, center, two wings and a rearguard.[8] It's almost funny. The image of them flexing their reedy muscles and strapping on their homemade gear, a bunch of skinny bricklayers pretending to be skilled in the art of battle—who were they trying to kid? What kind of enemy did they think they could overpower?

God knew they weren't going to strike fear in the hearts of savage armies by shaking their fists and slinging rocks. Besides, the battle they would ultimately be called upon to wage was to be a spiritual battle. They may have *thought* they were ready to take on all comers, but God knew their meeting with the Philistines would no doubt end in utter defeat and dissuade them from His purposes. And besides, there was a lot of preparation still to be done in their hearts and souls.

Even a full year later, in fact, they *still* weren't ready. At the fearsome sight of Canaan's inhabitants, they'd immediately say, "Let us appoint a leader and return to Egypt" (Num. 14:4). Well into the journey, the vast multitude (with the notable exception of two "one-in-a-millions") didn't want to move ahead with the kind of trust in Almighty God that would pulverize their enemies and sprout them up a new home in the Promised Land. God hadn't called them out of Egypt and into Canaan to achieve victories; He had called them to achieve intimacy.

You and I simply cannot know who we'd be if it weren't for the wilderness. We can't know for sure that we'd be bulwarks of faith and belief without spending some time in spiritual training. Even the great apostle Paul was dispatched to Arabia and other lonely places for three years after his dramatic conversion to Christ (see Gal. 1:15–18), where he got to know God in pivotal ways that would prepare him for his historic ministry to the first-century world—and to us. Peter certainly found himself stumbling and off balance in the wilderness after his denial of Christ, but this was valuable time if he was to become the firebrand preacher of Pentecost. John, late in life, was exiled on the island prison of Patmos—a wilderness if ever there was one, but apparently the ideal spot for God to reveal Himself in all His galloping glory.

From the dry, dusty middle of our wilderness, we may not be able to see any good reason for it or any good intentions on God's part for bringing us here. But again, figuring out the wilderness is not our job. If we'll just yield to God's purposes for us in the wilderness, He will protect us from ourselves and prepare us for our destiny.

## Things to Remember

The biblical account of the Hebrews' time spent in the wilderness gives us the benefit of getting a clearer view of God's purpose for the journey than they might have had. Fast-forwarding to the later years of their wilderness travel will be helpful as we gain insight in the midst of ours. Forty years into the journey, when Moses got the children of Israel to the brink of the Promised Land, he called them to a time of thinking back, remembering what they'd learned in the wilderness, and helping them get an answer to why God had allowed it.

> "Remember that the LORD your God led you on the entire journey
> these 40 years in the wilderness, so that He might humble you
> and test you to know what was in your heart, whether or not you
> would keep His commands." (Deut. 8:2 HCSB)

What had become clear from their forty years of wandering in the wilderness was that God had used it to "humble" them. Not to *humiliate* them as Egypt's Pharaoh had done but rather to strip away the pride that would keep them from being submissive, teachable people who could handle abundant living with gratitude and perspective. By humbling them, the true intentions of their hearts and their level of commitment to obedience would be revealed.

I'm sure you know of people who, after experiencing a visible taste of God's blessing in their lives, got to thinking they must have done something special to warrant His favor. I'm sure you've known times yourself when things were going pretty good for you, and you felt like you could ease up on your desperate feelings of dependence on God for a while. You could handle things from here. He could go help somebody else who needed Him more.

The wilderness is often God's reminder that we're not as big, strong, and independently capable as we think we are. Mothering small children has certainly brought this to the forefront in my own life during the past seven years. Let's just be honest: parts of the journey in motherhood are dry and dusty, but the tumbleweed blowing across the landscape of my daily, mundane demands has caused me to seek God with more fervor, to reach out to Him with more passion, to depend on Him with more consistency than ever before. Again and again, I'm humbled as I see my inability to handle daily demands, my bent toward impatience, and my need for divine stamina to keep up. Wilderness travel causes us never to wake up to a day when we're not totally in need of His love, provision, and care. It reminds us of the reality that even when we're the most healthy, the most self-disciplined, the most on top of our daily schedule, we're still living off His blessings. We're here because of Him. Sometimes the wilderness is what it takes to help us remember that.

And the Lord knows that being humbled will inevitably reveal to us who we really are and what's in the depths of our hearts. The wilderness is designed "to test you to know what is in your heart," which is a good thing to know now because it'll come in handy later.

Like any good teacher, God is wanting to find out if the facts we're learning are just a bunch of names and dates in our minds or if they're finally starting to come together in something that resembles understanding. He's wanting to see if we're making the leap from having His Word on the page to having His Word in our hearts, to see if all this pew-sitting is translating into pavement-walking.

I remember a particular season of life when our financial situation was particularly tenuous. The bills were coming in, and our income was just not keeping up. You probably know that sinking, scared feeling when it seems like the bottom is falling out from under your bank account. And whenever we'd talk about it, I'd complain to my husband about how hard it was to live under these conditions.

One day Jerry had listened to all the fussing he was going to take and bluntly said to me in his frustration, "Priscilla, are we going to trust God about this or not?" The starkness of his statement really took me back. I started to answer, but my man had me pegged. I could see so clearly now what was really lurking in my heart: ungratefulness and unbelief. I was failing the test.

God was allowing us to go through a patch of ground where the numbers on the spreadsheets weren't equaling the needs we had. This wasn't a mistake. This wasn't God being mean. This was a test to reveal what was in our hearts: trust or doubt.

We lie to ourselves so easily. We typically think of ourselves as above-average students, with pure hearts and clear motives. But we usually just want the cheapest and easiest route. We're not too keen on the development phase because we're really not all that interested in finding out the truth of who we are and having our hearts and minds genuinely molded to want what God wants.

Remember the Broadway play and children's movie *Annie*? When a reward was offered to her real parents if they would come and claim her from the orphanage, a couple posing as her mom and dad showed up to get their "daughter." But when she slowed them down from making a fast getaway by needing to stop and use the bathroom—(tell me little girls aren't good at that!)—their angry frustration revealed their true intentions. This first little snag in their plan revealed their true desires: they just wanted the money, not the girl. Like we just want the sweet family image, not the attention our children need when no one's watching. Like we just want the together professional image, not the discipline and homework it takes to have one. Like we just want the good church member image, not the repentance that's daily required of us if we want to worship with authentic reverence and desire.

Do we want the Promise Giver, or do we just want the Promised Land? The wilderness has a way of revealing our true intent, then leading us to love the former so we can genuinely experience the latter.

Finally, God employed the wilderness to see "whether or not you would keep His commands." Like it or not, obedience isn't hanging in our closet when we wake up in the morning, all starched and ironed and just begging to be put on. Obedience often has to be fished out of the dirty clothes pile. We have to look hard for it, like the matching sock that somehow got left out of the laundry. It's the choice between making what you have work or always needing something new from the store. Obedience takes effort.

And without the wilderness, we don't possess the muscle tone and endurance to try that hard. Without His fatherly willingness to stretch us and test us and prove us and strengthen us, we can't call up the courage to obey God even in the face of a challenge. As legendary British pastor and educator Charles Spurgeon said, the wilderness is "the Oxford and Cambridge for God's students. There they went to the University, and he taught and trained them, and they took their degree before they entered into the promised land."[9]

If you're in the wilderness asking, "Why me?" realize that there's a lot going on around you, among you, and within you that is taking you someplace. It's here that you get to know God more intimately than you've ever known Him before. It's here you experience a new level of trust, growing evermore confident that God will not let you be pressed "beyond what you are able" (1 Cor. 10:13). Here you develop the hard-won treasures of humility, authenticity, and obedience, becoming more prepared than ever to embrace fully the Promised Land life He has in store for you.

Don't spend all your energy trying to rush the wilderness or to wish it away. God is preparing you for Canaan. And once you're there, enjoying the abundance of His promises, experiencing Him in the fullness of joy, your humble, grateful, obedient heart will wonder in prayerful praise . . .

*Why me?*

*God can do anything, you know—far more than you could ever imagine or guess or request in your wildest dreams!*

EPHESIANS 3:20 *THE MESSAGE*

## CHAPTER 7

# Expect a Miracle

WE'D BEEN MARRIED ONLY THREE years, and our relationship was already in shambles. I couldn't talk to *him*. He couldn't talk to *me*. Every attempt at making things better just ended up in a full-scale argument. Honestly, we had more peace when we were apart from each other—with our own friends, doing our own thing—than we did when we were together. Ever been there?

My husband, preoccupied with the demands of a time-consuming job and other personal issues, had pretty much pushed me out of his life. I'd done the same thing to him, neglecting his needs and just expecting him to get over it. We'd been walking this thin emotional line for month after maddening month until marriage was no longer any fun for either of us. I was getting to the point—as I'd shared with one of my spiritual mentors on repeated occasions—where I was really close to just giving up.

And here we sat again, my wise friend and I, munching on a meal at one of our favorite local restaurants while I yakked, yakked, complained, complained. I could always count on her to be patient and understanding. She'd heard it all before, but she was always willing to listen.

On this particular day, however, she decided she was through just listening. Long-suffering soul that she is, it seemed shockingly out of character when she interrupted my rant by leaning back in her seat, exhaling a loud sigh, tapping an index finger against her lips, and staring back at me through eyes that let me know my blue-plate pity party was . . . well, done.

When she finally opened her mouth to speak, the words came out with the authority of God behind them. "Priscilla, you know I believe in miracles. In fact, I'm certain that one of the reasons for the wilderness seasons in our lives is to put us in a position where we'll start expecting more from God than we ever have before. I think it's time you stopped whining and complaining, girl, and started asking for—started anticipating!—God's supernatural activity."

Put *that* on your fork and eat it!

But, hey, she was right. I had found myself between a rock and a hard place. And like usual, I'd decided there was only so much that anybody could do about it. What I'd forgotten—again!—and what my mentor friend had boldly challenged me to remember was this: *the wilderness increases the opportunities to see God work miracles,* not just in some faraway place or for more deserving people. The wilderness opens the door for God to show His supernatural power right here, in my life—in your life.

In our experiences. In our emotions. In our emptiness.

## Nowhere to Turn

God can work a miracle in your experiences, you know.

Do you have a life experience or current circumstance in which you desperately need to see a miraculous move of God? The Israelites knew how you feel. They hadn't gotten very far out of Egypt before the Lord said to Moses, "Tell the sons of Israel to turn back and camp before Pi-hahiroth, between Migdol and the sea; you shall camp in front of Baal-zephon, opposite it, by the sea" (Exod. 14:2). Make that the Red Sea—the one that soon would become a chilling backdrop to one of the most impossible situations in all of human history.

When word came down of the Hebrews' location, Pharaoh realized that the wilderness had "shut them in" with no way of escape (v. 3). So with hundreds of Egyptian horsemen and chariots in tow, he led a mad dash to recapture his slave labor pool. And he found them where? "Beside Pi-hahiroth, in front of Baal-zephon" (v. 9), right where God had strategically placed them.

*This is just too easy,* Pharaoh must have thought. Like breaking a diet in the doughnut shop.

With the swirling waves of the Red Sea in their sight and Pharaoh's army closing in, the Israelites had a logical reaction to this kind of predicament, saying to Moses:

> Is it because there were no graves in Egypt that you have taken us away to die in the wilderness? Why have you dealt with us this way, bringing us out of Egypt? Is this not the word that we spoke to you in Egypt, saying, "Leave us alone that we may serve the Egyptians"? For it would have been better for us to serve the Egyptians than to die in the wilderness. (vv. 11–12)

And yet their logic was faulty in a number of ways and brimming over with sarcasm. Egyptian culture was enamored with death and the afterlife, its landscape littered with elaborate burial sites.[10]

So remembering Egypt as a nation without graves was simply an underhanded way of jabbing their leader. It was almost laughable. Plus, the way God had exacted the Israelites' release from Egypt could hardly have left the impression that they were out here by accident, simply to "die in the wilderness." All the frogs and hail and gnats and boils with which God had plagued the Egyptians—not once, not twice, but *ten times*—should have begun to build a track record with these people and their God. They should've had a steady confidence in Yahweh by now. The Red Sea wasn't the first experience they'd had where they needed God to perform a miracle to lead them to safety. They had seen their own families, in fact, spared from death while all the firstborn of Egypt, from every corner of the land, had fallen dead in one midnight hour. And this had happened just about a week beforehand!

But isn't that the way we usually are? We tend to forget the miraculous way God has dealt with us in the past—even the recent past— when a new experience presents itself that requires supernatural intervention. We fail to remember how His often unknown, unseen hand of protection and deliverance kept us going when we didn't think we could handle any more. We look back to a time before our problems reached such a danger point, before they turned into real emergencies, and we envy the seeming sense of ease we used to enjoy (forgetting that we complained just as hard then as we do now).

All we can feel are the walls closing in. All we can be sure of is that there's no way out. All we can see are the Egyptian hordes on one side and the vast Red Sea on the other.

The rock. The hard place.

But, my friend, this is God's place—the place where He wants to show His miracle-working power in your experience.

The Israelites' position at the lapping mouth of the Red Sea was no mistake. God knew they needed to see a mighty display of His power—one that would make a lasting impression on them, one that would be a visual reminder later on in their journey of exactly what He can do when all hope is gone. He wanted them in a place where the only available option was a miraculous move of God on their behalf, an incident that would serve as a bedrock of remembrance for the entire nation throughout the centuries to come.

"I would have despaired," David later wrote, "unless I had believed that I would see the goodness of the LORD in the land of the living" (Ps. 27:13). He had heard stories like these recounted to him. He had witnessed God's deliverance himself with his own eyes, in his own life. This is what our Red Sea circumstances are for—not to frustrate and discourage us, not to leave us writhing in despair, but rather to foster in us an enthusiasm and anticipation for what God is preparing to do: "the goodness of the Lord in the land of the living." In you. In me.

Are you in a Red Sea circumstance today? Are you caught between a rock and a hard place? Are you pinned against a decision that has to be made in the next forty-eight hours? Are you lost inside an impossibly complex problem without enough money to buy your way out of it and no good answers even if you did?

Then you're in a spot to be envied—like the Hebrews who were actually there when the waters of that sea piled up in a sloshing heap on either side of them. All we get to see is the 1950s movie version with Charlton Heston. Cool, but nothing like being there. Nothing like feeling the surge of adrenaline that coursed through their veins as they hightailed it across on dry land, looking down and seeing no mud collecting on their sandals. Nothing like watching four hundred years of Egyptian oppression being yanked to the sea floor by the undertow of God's almighty power.

Once you'd seen that, what else would you ever need to see again? Once you'd been rescued so miraculously from a life-or-death situation, you'd be expecting the unexpected every chance you got.

Right?

Well, for three days, maybe.

## Marah's Mirage

Granted, it was hot. Granted, there was no cable TV or clean linens waiting for them whenever they stopped for the night. Granted, drinkable water is heavy to carry. I've certainly noticed this myself when I've gone into the garage to bring in a big case of bottled water. It's a strain on your back and knees. And that's with the air conditioner going and a place to sit down afterwards.

But fresh on the back side of their spectacular deliverance at the Red Sea, after kicking up their heels in praise and celebration for nearly a solid chapter in Exodus 15, they took an eastward turn into the wilderness of Shur. And after only three days' walk, their water supplies were starting to wane with no supplemental sources in sight.

The problem seemed to be solved, however, when in verse 23, "they came to Marah," where the sight of available water brought a Red Sea skip back into their step—except for the fact that the water they found there was bitter, undrinkable, most likely filled with "salt, minerals, and perhaps even poison."[11] Imagine the peoples' frustration and disgust when after slogging three hot days in the semiarid wilderness, after plunging toward the watering hole that seemed to contain God's great provision, they spit it out of their mouths. Too gross to drink. Even for somebody dying of thirst.

Why would God pour a glass of undrinkable water in front of a dehydrated crowd?

Crystal asked a question like that not long ago. A spunky, smart, articulate thirty-one-year-old, she had recently completed her MBA program. This left her with high expectations for increasing her job prospects, walking into an exciting, opportunity-laden career. Her university professors and past employers had filled her reference sheet with glowing reports on her ability, her attitude, her assets to any company that was lucky enough to hire her. The interview process went a little slow, as it often can. Initial assurances followed by timing delays followed by promising signals followed by let's-talk-again-next-week. But the day finally came when the caller on the other end of the line was making a job offer. An excellent job offer. She might even call it her dream job. "Can you start in two weeks?"

But two days before she was scheduled to begin—after lots of exciting celebration and a fair amount of new wardrobe shopping—a neatly typed letter arrived in the afternoon mail. It seems her new company had been bought by a major affiliate, a transaction that had been in the works for some time but had just now become official. This new development would mean some changes in the department she was to work in. Her position had been eliminated. Her job offer was being retracted.

Nearly every wilderness journey has a Marah moment—a place where you're certain that refreshment is just around the bend. Everything has been coming together. The ideal environment has been created. Your long-sought-after help is sure to arrive. You've been hot, tired, and frustrated. You've groaned and griped yourself to sleep for long enough now. You've decided you can hold out until this moment—the time when it appears the right amount of money is finally going to come in, when the relief you need is finally going to show up, when the answer is finally going to be yes.

Any day now your boyfriend is going to pop the question. The doctor has said this remedy is almost certain to be the cure for your ailment. Your spouse is giving every indication that he is finally back, both physically and emotionally. The promotion you've been waiting for is within days of being yours. Your investment broker assures you that the chance you took last quarter is going to pay off in this one.

Ahh . . . a cool drink in the midst of a hot journey.

So you run headlong, ready to dive into the supposed certainty of God's deliverance. You've been praying for this. You've been watching things happening. This has got to be the answer! Gotta be!

Then at the last minute your promotion goes to someone else. Divorce papers are delivered to your door. You're in the 1 percent of people whose body rejects this particular form of medication. Stock prices tumble. Your fiancée decides to call the whole thing off. Marah's waters have proven to be only a mirage of fulfillment. They didn't satisfy like you thought they would.

Here you sit disappointed. Again.

## Emotional Healing

God can work a miracle in your emotions, you know.

If you've been nodding your head with me these last few paragraphs, quickly put yourself into one or more of these scenarios. If you know exactly what I mean when I talk about Marah moments, then you also know how bitter water can turn into a bitter heart at times like these, crush your spirit, and ruin your resolve. When you've been disappointed by others, when you've become frustrated with God for leading you to a place where there's nothing to quench your thirst, you can brim over like the waters of Marah with poisonous bitterness. Marah's mirage can leave your heart angry and calloused.

There was a rock. There was a hard place. And now an unjust, unfair place.

But still, this is God's place.

God's goal for our journey is not only that we see His power at work in our *experiences*, as He proved at the Red Sea, as He's proven in your own life when things looked black and He brought them to life again. He also wants us to see His miraculous power at work in our *emotions*. That's why when Moses cried out to God, and God showed him a tree, Moses "threw it into the waters, and the waters became sweet" (v. 25). In one swift move of vulnerability and obedience, Moses found God ready to act, relieving both the peoples' thirst and their tired emotions. That which was bitter had been made sweet.

Are you bitter because of the hand you've been dealt? Sometimes He'll allow us to come face-to-face with an experience that could potentially breed bitterness, just so we can see His ability to work miracles in the way we feel. He wants us to know that our natural slide into bitterness and anger can be caught by the rescuing hand of His grace, then transformed into a state of mind, mood, and motivation that could only come from the Lord Himself. One word from God, and the bitter can become sweet, my friend. And when the day comes that you can look up from a Marah moment with hope, gratitude, and—even after all this—a hearty expectation that God can still do the unexpected, you'll know you haven't acquired these confident feelings by your own sturdy bootstraps. They're yours only by the supernatural power of God, performing a miracle in your emotions.

Only God can bring a smile to the face of one who's going through a bitter divorce.

Only God can call up a sigh of relief from the dry mouth of one who's fighting disease.

Only God can usher peace into the heart of one who's brokenhearted over a wayward son.

Only God can quiet the screeching fears of one whose worries are keeping her up all night.

Only God can stir feelings of confident contentment in one whose financial condition is in peril.

So when Moses, who was just as thirsty as everyone else, either tasted the bitter water himself or heard the raucous complaining of the crowd, he didn't shake his fist at such bad misfortune. He knew how to handle bitterness. His first response was to cry out to the Lord, the only place he knew his help could come from.

"And the LORD showed him a tree" (Exod. 15:25).

Now if Moses had gone to throwing things, if he had joined the crowd in wanting to go back for some of that decent drinking water they had in Egypt, if he was fed up with having to live with all these challenges one after the other, he might have missed the miracle God was waiting to perform. We can sometimes get so focused on this one thing, this one way we're wanting God to act on our behalf, this one moment when He's supposed to show up and do something spectacular, that we close ourselves off from His greater purposes.

This all comes from trying to *fix* the wilderness rather than *yield* to the wilderness. Sometimes the better thing God is wanting to do just needs to be waited on for a little while longer. Maybe ten days, maybe even ten months or ten years, or—in the Hebrews' case— maybe about ten minutes.

When you've faced a true disappointment, when bitterness keeps wanting to cloak itself around your shoulders, growing harder and harder for you to shake off, take a cue from Israel's leader and cry out to God in the midst of your struggle. And even if He knows in His own sovereign will that it's not yet time to work a miracle in your experience, He will assure you it's time to let Him work a miracle in your emotions. He'll show you, just as He did Moses, exactly what to do to take that huge heartache of yours and—believe it or not—turn it into a sweet spot that daily reminds you how big and strong and powerful your God really is.

Sometimes what we need most is not a change of circumstances; sometimes what we need most is a change of heart. And when He does that, when He rescues us from our usual routine of anger and revenge and gossip and bitterness, we don't just need to be glad about it for now. We need to remember it the next time our emotions are pressing down hard on us, luring us, wanting us. We need to remember God's track record so we'll feel more confident about trusting Him when we start to get thirsty again.

Or hungry.

## Heaven's Pantry

God can work a miracle in your emptiness, you know.

This wilderness walk with God is supposed to help us see that what He can accomplish in one area of our lives also applies in another. In fact, it applies in *all* the others. God had "tested" the people at the bitter waters of Marah (Exod. 15:25), and before too many weeks had passed, He decided to "test them" again (16:4)—this time in culinary school.

Remember, they had likely been planning for something like a thirty-day trip from Egypt to Canaan. So when the thirty- to forty-day mark arrived and they were nowhere nearer the milk and honey, it's not hard to imagine that their food supply was dwindling. What they could supply for themselves had waned, and they'd wound up empty. Wonder if God had accounted for this when He decided to send them the opposite direction of the place they were trying to reach?

Earlier they had gotten thirsty, and God had provided what they needed. Now that they were starting to experience hunger, would they bank on Him to provide for their needs, based on His track record of faithfulness, or . . .

Not.

"Would that we had died by the LORD's hand in the land of Egypt, when we sat by the pots of meat, when we ate bread to the full" and yada, yada, yada (v. 3). We've heard all of this before. To hear them say it, God had brought them out here to kill them, as if the Egyptians hadn't been doing a pretty good job of that for generations.

But even in growing exasperated at them, can't we see a big dose of ourselves in their words and reactions? God had shown Himself strong in their *experience* at the Red Sea. He had shown Himself strong in their *emotions* at Marah three days later. "Yeah, that was pretty good how You did all of that back there, God, but now we're hungry. This is something new, something we haven't faced before, something else that's different from what you've bailed us out of before. I don't see how in the world You can do anything about *this!*"

You wait. He can show Himself strong in your *emptiness*.

So what do you do when the person, place, or thing you thought would keep you filled no longer satisfies? What do you do when your career turns lackluster, when your marriage becomes mundane, when your children are draining you dry, when the ladder of success you've been climbing is leaned up against the wrong wall, when religion is wearing you out?

Just as clearly as you recognize your stomach's call for suppertime, you will undergo seasons when you feel empty—spiritually, mentally, physically. Everything you'd brought along to take care of this—your churchgoing, your do-gooding, your read-through-the-Bible plan—it's all starting to feel dry and unappetizing. You're worn out and famished, even in the midst of doing exactly what God has called and led you to do during this period of life.

I'm not telling you to hold back from living day to day with faithfulness and devotion. But there are times when nothing will satisfy—no matter how hard you try to manufacture fullness—until God starts raining down "bread from heaven for you" (16:4). Oh yes, God accounted for this when He sent you the opposite direction into that wilderness. He knew your supply would run dry. So not every feeling of emptiness is the result of your doing something wrong. Not every growl in your spiritual stomach comes from being faithless or from doing things in the wrong order. Sometimes it's just a test to see what (to see Who) you're really counting on to keep you satisfied, an opportunity for Him to show you His supernatural, miraculous power in your emptiness.

When the Israelites came to their place of physical emptiness in the wilderness of Sin, between Elim and Mount Sinai (which is just a geographical name, not a metaphor for the "sin" in their lives), God met them with the superabundance of His provision. Why? Because they were handling themselves so perfectly, so beautifully? Obviously not. His reason for showering them in manna from heaven was so they would "know that I am the LORD your God" (v. 12).

Are you feeling starved for relationship? Do you feel like you're just wasting away inside without a boyfriend, a marriage partner? Is church-as-usual becoming increasingly less satisfying for you? Can no amount of conferences and Bible studies keep your energy up for very long anymore? God is calling you to His kitchen. He is wanting to open wide His pantry for you. And if you're yielding to the wilderness rather than fighting it, you will find His table spread with provisions that will keep you fed from day to day through the dry spells.

Oh yes, start anticipating miracles.

Welcome the rocks and the hard places.

Expect breakthrough at Marah's mirage.

Lay out a place setting at an empty table.

Expect the unexpected. And be filled from on high.

*They will not hunger or thirst, neither will mirage [mislead]
or scorching wind or sun smite them; for He Who has mercy
on them will lead them, and by springs of water will He guide
them.*

ISAIAH 49:10 AMP

CHAPTER 8

# From Why to How

SHANA'S BEEN A FRIEND FOR more than a decade. And through the
last four or five of those years, she's been a wilderness traveler. Who'd
have seen it coming? She'd been a bright, cheerful, expressive, young
pastor's wife, managing life inside the church bubble with grace, wit,
and charm. But things went spiraling downhill fast, beginning with
the untimely death of her husband. Upon his passing, the church
in which they had faithfully invested themselves began to ostracize
her. She tried to endure—tried to be a good soldier—but with her
emotions understandably fragile, she finally felt forced to relocate
to another city where she's continued to battle relentless waves of
loneliness and depression.

Her search to find fulfilling work at this early, unexpected stage
of widowhood has proven mostly fruitless. In basically every area of

her life, she keeps running into one brick wall after another. Attempts at coping have led her to make a series of poor decisions, some that she's just too ashamed to talk about. When we spoke by phone the other day, I could almost feel her body trembling as her words shook with a volatile mixture of shame and desperation. "I feel so alone, Priscilla. Does God remember me at all anymore? I just need to know He's still there, and I need to know how to make it through this journey."

*I need to know how . . .*

This question resonated with me because it's what we're all wondering: "How does God expect me to traverse this wilderness?" When I think of Shana, I realize again that the wilderness is no light subject to be addressing. Calling this the "development" phase is not intended as a way of reducing it down to mechanical steps and quick fixes. This is serious. Yours may be *extremely* serious. I don't want to give any impression that some three-point outline is all that's standing between you and sweet relief. Your God knows the depth of your pain and heartache. He knows the tears you cry when no one is watching. He sees you, my friend, and has not forgotten or forsaken you, even if your suffering is more acute than it's ever been before. "From the end of the earth I call to You," David said (Ps. 61:2)—from the end of your rope, from the end of your strength. Even here, even now, in your season of desperate longing, your precious Lord is here to hold you, to be your strong rock and refuge.

At the same time, as I've said before, the wilderness can be—as it is for me at this moment—simply a season of time that you're struggling to enjoy. Maybe you find yourself often feeling frustrated and fatigued, not to mention guilty for finding reasons to complain amid such obvious blessings. Yet even then, it can still lead us to cry out, "How do I keep my sense of purpose up when I can feel myself wearing down?" Even when we've begun to get a handle on some of the reasons *why* He might allow the wilderness, we still want to know *how* we can make it through.

I'll just admit again—as much as I adore my three boys and am deliriously thankful to God for them, this journey through parenting young children is not a walk in the park for me. I'm enjoying it more as they get older, but the baby phase wears me out! To be the kind of mom I desire to be, I continually have to ask God to empower me.

To make matters worse, I have a sister who was made for mother-hood. She does it so well, with patience and a settled peace about this season in her journey. I think it's fair to say that she was just born with the mothering gene. She has five children, and the last three have been birthed at home with the assistance of a midwife. (Sigh.) I've been there rooting her on, right by her side, for all but the last one—when I was home recuperating from the hospital birth of my third son. (I admire her, but as for me and my house, we will have an epidural.)

When her babies begin to gravitate toward solid food, she only lets them eat things that have been puréed fresh by her, by hand. (Another sigh.) Gerber's just not good enough. When they begin growing toward school age, she teaches them their lessons at home. And loves it! (Yet another sigh.) She's been thinking about, planning for, and looking ahead to these years her whole life.

But being brutally honest here, motherhood is something I've had to grow into. Something that I'm still growing into. The per-son who said motherhood is a journey out of selfishness certainly knew what she was talking about. There are days when I wonder how I'm going to make it through this without losing what's left of my sanity.

Not too long ago our whole family was in the car on our way to someplace. Jerry was driving, talking on his cell phone. (You're still allowed to do that in Texas.) The boys were in the backseat, kicking up enough noise and chaos to power a small village. And I was in the front seat, staring blankly out the passenger window.

Have you ever done that? Stared blankly while your life, with all its spinning parts, whirled around you in a chaotic fury? Have you ever thought to yourself, *How did we get here? How did this happen?* That's how I felt on this particular day.

And yet, as I watched the trees and traffic and telephone poles go by, I was surprised to find myself humming. Just singing a little song. And as the words and tune reverberated in my head, I suddenly had a flashback to my own mother, sitting in her own front seat, while her own children—my three siblings and I—were riding in the back, nudging and poking and antagonizing one another. In one of those random images that had somehow embedded itself in my long-term memory, I could see the back of her head. I could see her staring out the window. And I could hear her humming. Just singing a little song, like I was doing now.

And now I knew why. She was trying to hold on to her sanity. And God was giving her a song to help her do it.

God told His people through the prophet Hosea:

> Behold, I will allure her, bring her into the wilderness, and speak kindly to her. Then I will give her vineyards from there, and the valley of Achor as a door of hope. And she will sing there as in the days of her youth, as in the day when she came up from the land of Egypt. (Hosea 2:14–15)

You've got to be kidding! Kindness and vineyards and hope and singing . . . while in the *wilderness?* The wilderness seasons—no matter how grim, chaotic, or relatively generic—are filled with questions, upsetting circumstances, even doubts about what God is thinking or why He's lost the directions to your house and your needs. But according to the prophet Hosea, our God is powerful enough to produce vineyards in this dry, dusty soil. He's able to put an ironic, illogical smile on your face when hope looks like nothing but a closed door. He's even able to put a song in your heart that seems to have no business being there.

When the time is just right—and in a way only He can—He comes to show us *how* He'll enable us to handle our wilderness walk.

## $500 Stories

My mother was a twenty-something seminary wife with two toddlers, trying her best to manage in a makeshift apartment in a bad part of town. She'd been a good sport. She'd stopped being startled at the roaches that scurried out from the baseboards. She'd learned to make do with what little they had. But one late afternoon, throwing open the empty cupboards to see what kind of magic she could work on the evening's dinner, the bare bones and bean cans stared back at her in all their unimagination. Why they seemed more tasteless and unappetizing today than they had for all the weeks and months before, she couldn't really say. But for whatever reason, the sight of beans, beans, and more beans caused tears to start pooling in her eyes. By the time my daddy got home, the pools had reached flood stage.

She was just flat-out tired of this life. So was he. Mom didn't mean to make him feel bad for forcing his family to brave these kinds of conditions. She wasn't questioning the call God had on his life as he studied in seminary. It's just that on this night, at this moment, the bean cans had come crashing down all around her. And if she couldn't come up with, I don't know, $500 to get some food in the house and a few other necessities in place, she didn't see herself marshalling the strength to make it through.

Five hundred dollars. When Dad asked her how much she thought they needed, that's the round figure that popped into her mind. Five hundred dollars. Which may as well have been five million, as far as their meager prospects were concerned. But sitting there on their spindly sticks of furniture, beans simmering on the stove, that's what they cried out to God for as they held each other close and tried to hang on.

The next day—I know you've heard stories like these before, but they happen; they do—Dad turned the key to his campus mailbox, where resting inside was a money order for (oh yeah) . . . $500. It had come out of the blue from the middle of nowhere and had landed smack-dab in the middle of their wilderness. God hadn't forgotten them. And they had $500 to prove it.

You may think these stories exist only in sermons. But I'll bet if you'd open your eyes and look around the place you're in, this wilderness God's led you to, you'd spot at least one reason for being thankful. You'd recognize a touching example of God's disaster unit ministering to your needs out here in the dry and dusty. Think back and remember. Even if you've forgotten or were honestly too bummed to notice at the time, I'll bet you've got a $500 story of your own that could be told.

They don't even have to be that expensive.

I remember oversleeping one day, too late to have my quiet time or get any exercise, just feet-hit-the-floor, kids-need-their-mommy. Jerry had needed to head out early so I was all alone with the break-fast brigade. "You boys want some eggs?" I asked, opening the fridge. Hold on, no eggs. *Pancakes?* I pulled out the batter and a mixing bowl, and then remembered—*no eggs.* Right. *Cereal?* Swinging the refrigera-tor door open yet again, I saw that someone had left about an eighth of a teaspoon of milk in the jug. Wait till I get my hands on the guy who did that!

So breakfast that morning was the last two slices of wheat bread, toasted, with jam and (if my boys knew what was good for them) no complaints.

I had a whole bunch of errands to run that morning, but we weren't going anywhere till I could get everybody dressed. I hadn't washed clothes all week. I think everybody ended up with at least one item pulled straight from the hamper. And it only got worse. We were late for every appointment. Every line was longer than the last. By the time we finally made it back home that afternoon, I threw my keys on the table, plopped my purse on the floor, sent the little ones to their room, and sent me to mine.

And there it was—like a shaft of sunshine and an angel chorus singing in the background. On the nightstand sat a huge bouquet of gorgeous flowers, a note tucked gently into the arrangement. Opening it, I read these simple words from my husband, the milk bandit—

"Just because."

A little refreshment just in the nick of time. My husband did it for me during a tough day and God will do it for us during tough seasons.

God's not one to leave us without any hope. How does He expect you to make it? He brings bits of refreshment along, just when He knows you need them.

## Enough to Match Your Need

They came to Elim where there were twelve springs of water and seventy date palms, and they camped there beside the waters. (Exod. 15:27)

Elim was the most extensive watercourse in the area, estimated to be about a mile wide, an oasis adorned with a great variety of trees. Imagine the thirsty, discouraged Hebrews squinting through the blurry haze of sand, seeing in the distance what appeared to be a palm tree. Imagine how the buzz of surprise must have spread through the ranks when, not just one, but *dozens* of trees were spotted. Palm trees meant nearby water, and nearby water meant these thirsty travelers had refreshment waiting on them just beyond the next rise. It must have seemed like a love letter sent to them straight from God.

An oasis.

In the wilderness.

And this is what makes a wilderness different from a desert. A desert is nothing more than a barren expanse of sand dunes that can't support wildlife or vegetation. A wilderness may certainly have long, arid regions like that, but the withering dryness is sprinkled at various places with springs and oases. Here and there grassy upland plains form a restful contrast to the rugged, inhospitable wasteland below. Although there were stretches of travel in the Israelites' journey where refreshment seemed scarce, their particular wilderness contained lush oases like that of Kadesh in the north, as well as the Wadi Feran near Sinai in the south, plus various brooks to break up the dryness. God's people might have died if He had marooned them in the desert, but no, He had led them into the wilderness, where just-in-time refreshment was at least occasionally on tap. God doesn't lead His people to a place where survival is not possible but rather to a stretch of land where they can be sustained. Thank God for choosing to allow wilderness travel for you and me, forgoing the road through the desert.

Look, in fact, at how precise God's provision was. "Twelve springs of water" to match the twelve tribes of Israel. What a great illustration of God's overwhelming care and specific concern for His people. He knows *exactly* what it takes to refresh you. When He chooses to encourage your heart with a dose of divine comfort, it won't look like what He gives to somebody else. You can be sure it's what He *knows* will be just the right amount and quality to refuel your tanks and recharge you for the journey. Whether it's a hug given at just the right moment, a word spoken in due season, an unexpected card or e-mail, or a conference that refreshes you with fellowship and messages that seem to have your name on them, it'll be a $500 story uniquely designed for you—to keep you going when you don't think you can.

Please don't miss Him when He comes by to offer an "Elim" to you as you trudge along.

And don't lose track of the times He already has.

I'll tell you what I do so I don't forget. I keep a little Microsoft Word file going on my computer, a document I've entitled "He Speaks to Me." When God communicates something to me through the Word, through a message, through conversation with a friend, or just by a thought that comes directly from His Spirit, I write it down in that spot. Any bit of encouragement that strengthens me on my journey gets recorded in this space. When He does something that is obviously from His hand—when it's clear that this is no coincidence, that this is not an occurrence that just accidently happened—I type it up for safekeeping. I want to remember. I want to be able to look back. I don't want to forget.

I was looking through my file recently and came across one of the more awesome incidents from a number of years ago when we were needing to find some office space for our ministry. As Jerry and I had been praying, we'd found a piece of property that was ideal for what we needed, situated in the area of town we sensed God was leading us to operate out of. But it was really more than we could afford. *Way* more. As you know, however, when you start feeling that God is involved in something, you don't want to let the usual obstacles be the final, determining factors. While the property stayed available, we kept praying. Kept waiting to see what might happen to make it reality.

Circumstances finally converged until we were forced to make a yes-or-no decision within a matter of days on acquiring this piece of real estate. We prayed for God to give us clear direction. The deadline followed a weekend when I would be speaking at a conference. And near the end of the event, a woman I had never seen or met before rushed up and said, "I know you don't know who I am, but a mutual friend of ours told me that you were interested in some land in the area where I live. In fact, the property you're looking at is basically adjacent to the property we own. We're about to put ours up for sale, and as I've been sitting here this weekend, I believe the Holy Spirit has said to me that we need to do whatever it takes to make sure this property we have is yours."

I'm not even going to tell you how it all worked out. That would muddy the point. All that matters is this: God had gone out of His way to bring a woman I had never met to an event where I happened to be speaking, who happened to live on the same street where the property we were considering was located. And I knew from the moment she made her unexpected offer to me, it was irrelevant whether or not the deal actually came together. God had used this experience to remind me, "Priscilla, I've got your back. You're on My mind. What concerns you concerns Me. I care about the little things as well as the big things. Don't you worry. I will take care of you."

That story still "speaks to me" of God's goodness. And recalling it helps me to keep pressing forward.

## More than a Miracle

Real-life stories like the one I just mentioned don't happen every day in anyone's life. The oases and streams the children of Israel encountered were spaced along on their journey. These people didn't have Red Sea crossings every afternoon. Stunning events in their lives that are separated by only a handful of verses in our Bibles were often weeks, months, even years apart. But we know from Scripture—as we've seen before—that they did have a daily reminder of God's living presence with them, His ongoing answer to their "how" questions:

> The Lord was going before them in a pillar of cloud by day to
> lead them on the way, and in a pillar of fire by night to give them
> light, that they might travel by day and by night. He did not take
> away the pillar of cloud by day, nor the pillar of fire by night, from
> before the people. (Exod. 13:21–22)

In a manner that was unprecedented in Hebrew history, God chose to reveal Himself to His people—day after day, night after night—through a visible manifestation of His presence. This is called a *theophany,* a theological term used to describe a God appearance, when He assumed a form and supernaturally revealed Himself within the natural realm of Earth. Even in the darkest moments of their journey—throughout the entire forty years—they could step out of their tents, look His direction, and catch an inspiring glimpse of His nearness, His hovering protection. Though they were walking blind through unknown, uncharted territory, they could count on God's fire and cloud to show them exactly where He wanted them to go.

Many theories have been offered by scholars for how this cloud was caused. They've suggested that it was simply caused by a nasty case of bad weather. But I've never heard of a storm cloud lasting forty years. Others say it was the natural dust the Israelites kicked up as they slogged along. But they weren't always on the move. Indeed, there is no other plausible explanation for the duration and dependability of this fire/cloud combination than that God was supernaturally behind it. These were physical pictures of His guiding presence, His way of bringing tangible evidence of Himself to His children.

Wouldn't that be awesome to have when we're wondering how we can continue to make it through our own wilderness? Wouldn't my friend Shana be encouraged if she could look up and see God showing her the next step to take as she journeys out of loss and despair? Wouldn't it be cool if God would just come down and linger over the house He wants you to buy, over the church He wants you to attend, over the person He wants you to date and marry? Even if His answers weren't that specific and precise, the simple fact that He was there, hanging right over the roofline, stationed directly over the back porch, would encourage us that He hadn't forgotten us. It would give us the encouragement we needed to make it through to the end. We'd wake up in the morning and know for sure He had plans for us through the day.

But, hey, we've *got* that.

Though God temporarily used theophanies throughout Old Testament times, He now deposits Himself within believing hearts through His ever-living, ever-present Holy Spirit. And if that sounds like some kind of cop-out compared to what the Israelites had—second fiddle to something we could see with our eyes, something we could confirm by asking our next-door neighbor if she saw it too—we're selling the Holy Spirit way short, just the way our enemy would want us to. The Holy Spirit is the most supernatural phenomenon we could ever imagine.

And while He is invisible, He is "God with us" and, I believe, wants to manifest His presence in our lives in a visible way. Just as the children of Israel could catch sight of God outside their tent doors, we can have God sightings of our own as the Holy Spirit opens our spiritual eyes to recognize His activity around us. Would you consider that an unexpected phone call that changed everything for you or even just lifted you out of the evening's doldrums wasn't coincidence but was God demonstrating His very real presence to you? What about when the taste and desire you had for that addictive behavior was totally removed from your palate? Could you see the cloud of His presence when that stranger said exactly what you needed to hear, when your financial need was met at the last minute, or when the e-mail popped up in your in-box offering to give you the help you needed? What about when, after endless sleepless nights pondering what to do, you just "knew" the right decision to make?

Friend, it wasn't luck. It wasn't coincidence. It was God. In your life, right here and right now.

I know how it happens, though. I know how it feels to sit on that pew, hearing all those things about God but doubting they really happen in a person's actual day. I know how to skim over all those Scriptures that talk about how the Spirit can "guide you into all the truth," how He can "speak" where we can hear Him, how He can "disclose to you what is to come" (John 16:13). Shucks, I know how to read, but I don't always know how to *believe*—to believe that these might really be things I could expect to experience.

I've spent too many years in the cozy comfort zones of Christianity, settling down where it's just safer not to expect much out of God. But He is starting to show me, by His kind and patient grace, that He desires to reveal Himself to me in ways every bit as real and visible as His obvious nearness was to the Hebrew wanderers. And though He's shown me a lot, I don't think I've seen anything yet! And the more my eyes are opened to see Him, the more encouraged I am to make it through this wilderness.

## How Now

When we find ourselves in the wilderness, the most common questions we ask—after the whys—are often the hows. How does God expect us to handle this? How are we supposed to keep going? How do we know what to do when every decision seems like it leads to a dead end or perhaps even worse.

A big part of the answer to questions like these is found less in *how* we do it than in *what* God has done to make the *how* possible— what He has done already, as well as what He's presently doing.

That's why a $500 story is so invaluable. It's the kind of story that no one can take away from you or convince you it was mere coincidence—because you were *there*. You know for a fact how dire the need was and how impossible a solution seemed. You remember how tired and thirsty you were and how good that drink of cool water tasted on parched lips. You can still hear the person's voice when he called to say that the situation had changed and he thought he really would have a job for you. You can still see the look on your spouse's face when the accountant said there'd been a mistake on your tax return, and you not only owed less than you thought, but they even owed you a refund. You can still feel the tingle that raced down your spine when you asked the Lord to give you some proof that He cared, not ten minutes before running into an old school friend in the DMV line who told you how often she'd thought of you over the years and that nobody had influenced her ability to trust God more than you had.

I know this journey you're traveling may be hard and long and seemingly unending. But remember, this is not a desert; it's a wilderness. There's a big difference. Refreshment can be found along these roads. His Spirit is always with you—guiding you, leading you, communicating with you, directing you in the Father's will. And if you'll keep trusting and keep watching, yielding to His direction, He will even surprise you now and then with some strategically placed, sovereignly created Elims of refreshment. It'll be exactly what you need. And it'll keep you going when you think you can't.

His Spirit is with you—believe it!—doing what only He can do so that you can do what He is showing you. He is your ever-present enabler. So ask Him. Ask Him to open your eyes to see His "what" so that you can get an answer to your "how."

*I would have despaired unless I had believed that I would see the goodness of the LORD in the land of the living. Wait for the LORD. Be strong and let your heart take courage; Yes, wait for the LORD.*

PSALM 27:13–14

## CHAPTER 9

# In Between

ELIM COMES. AND ELIM GOES.

And then what?

> They set out from Elim and all the congregation of the sons of Israel came to the wilderness of Sin, which is *between* Elim and Sinai. (Exod. 16:1, author italics)

God had evidenced His love and provision for His children at Elim by providing much-needed refreshment. And not too long in the future, He would wow them again at Sinai. But the passage from one miraculous moment with God to the next required a journey that would take them "in between."

No doubt this travel between Elim and Sinai in the wilderness of Sin would have covered nothing more than barren and dry territory that left much to be desired. They'd be put to the task of plodding along while staring at endless acres of vast wasteland under the blazing hot sun. And yet this part of the journey was necessary if they were to come to the next place where God's glory would visibly and tangibly be displayed. The "in between" down time wasn't a waste. It was a bridge between one stunning moment with God and the next.

For about a three-year period in Jerry's and my recent past, God was on somewhat of a hit parade, a Holy Ghost highlight reel. Just about any time we found ourselves in real need of things, God would supernaturally provide them. When I made a specific request involving the birth of one of our sons, He followed through as if I had called in a made-to-order pizza. The way this was going, I thought I might never have to park more than three or four spaces away from the grocery store entrance ever again.

My prayer times were rich and vibrant. The Word seemed almost to sparkle in my hands, exploding with deep, personal insight and revelation. I had never known a season of greater intimacy and excitement with the Lord. It was absolutely incredible!

Then, like a sunset slowly fading away, my journal entries seemed to disappear behind the back side of the moon. There was nothing extraordinary to report. I was still praying, still studying, still doing all the same stuff. Only now it felt like I was in a vacant room, like someone who's still carrying on the remnants of a conversation, not realizing that the person you were just talking to had left.

My spiritual disciplines became more of a chore, a duty, an effort. When I did make the time to be quiet before Him, I was much more anxious to cut the whole thing short. It didn't feel like we were connecting like we used to, which left me easily distracted and ready to move on to something else. He just wasn't knocking my socks off anymore, and I wasn't sure why. What had changed? What had happened?

It was hard not to complain about it. Honestly, that's what those in-between times often entice me to do. Seems like the Israelites had the same struggle, for when they found themselves between Elim and whatever was next, "the whole congregation of the sons of Israel grumbled against Moses and Aaron in the wilderness" (Exod. 16:2).

Some lessons apparently can take thousands of years to learn.

Perhaps the one thing we know best about the ancient Hebrews, especially during their forty years of wandering, was their penchant for complaining. In between miracles, when the business of the day was primarily just to wait and walk and obey, they could quickly begin doubting God's love for them. They doubted His power to counteract the challenging situations they faced. If He wasn't parting the Red Sea, or sweetening the bitter waters of Marah, or sprouting palm trees out of Elim's nowhere, these people weren't likely to be happy. Their contentment and satisfaction seemed to rise and fall based on whether or not God was amazing them at the moment.

I easily qualify as one who relates. When the dry, dusty wilderness starts to stretch out as far as the eye can see on all four sides, when the refreshment of Elim is no longer dripping off my tongue and Mount Sinai's peak is not yet in view, when no sign of God's presence or miraculous intervention is anywhere in sight, I'm one of the first to start thinking sour thoughts. Patience is not my strong suit. And those long in-between periods know just how to play me.

Sometimes God goes silent. But that's no reason to start making so much noise.

## Another Train of Thought

I hope you've seen enough of me in this book to know that I can't speak on the subject of complaining without needing to give myself a good talking-to as well. Anything good that grows in me is purely a result of God taking charge and making it happen. Left to myself, I'm right there with the "no one who does good, not even one" crowd (Ps. 53:3).

But this complaining business—I'll just say it—it's ugly.

Each time we see the Israelites murmuring and complaining, it's worse than the time before. At first it's just the "people" doing the fussing (Exod. 15:24). Then it's "all the congregation of the sons of Israel" (16:1). They go from just grousing to Moses alone, to taking their complaint to both Moses and Aaron. That's the pattern of complaining—always intensifying, always escalating. It starts with a few minor, incidental frustrations, then builds over time into a wildfire, whipped into flame by every available draft of oxygen. Everything becomes a new subject for its scorn—Exhibits X, Y, and Z in an ever-growing list of grievances. With the door blown open that wide, there's not much to stop the griping or even to slow it down. How quickly it becomes our preferred way of going in and out. How much easier it gets to bemoan our fate than to engage our faith.

But make no mistake: a grumbling spirit will rob you and me of the treasures God is seeking to refine in us out here in the wilderness. It will slow our progress. It will hinder our readiness for the Promised Land. Choosing not to honor God or to give Him thanks during the in-between times causes us not only to waste His better purposes but also allows our "foolish heart" to grow "darkened" (Rom. 1:21). That's right, an "unthankful heart eventually becomes dark."[12] Remaining unresponsive to God's goodness and activity results in a form of spiritual blindness, one that persists even when He begins to operate again in visible, vocal ways.

Several years ago Jerry and I flew to Memphis for a speaking event. A nice woman from the church there picked us up at the airport and drove us to the hotel where we'd be staying. Dropping us off, she said, "Listen, I live here in the neighborhood. So if you need anything, just give me a holler. Otherwise, I'll see you first thing in the morning."

It wasn't late at all when we got there—just about 7:30—but it had been a really long week and we were utterly exhausted. All we wanted was to locate the bed and fall asleep in it. Before 8:00 had even rolled around, we were stretched out, under the covers, out till morning.

Make that 10:00 p.m.

People often say a tornado sounds like a freight train. I don't know for sure. But I do know what a freight train sounds like at 10:00 at night, in an unfamiliar town, when you're dead asleep and it's the last thing you're expecting. It sounds like a tornado's hit. Right there in your hotel room.

Jerry and I sat bolt upright for at least sixty long seconds, trying to figure out if we were in an earthquake or perhaps downstairs from a vacuum cleaner convention. Finally the roaring trailed away into the Memphis night, off to terrorize some other poor sleeping souls. Dazed but still able to shake it off, we were soon nestled back into sleep.

Until 1:00 a.m.

It was back.

By this wee time of morning, I was evangelistically ticked off. I threw back the blankets, stumbled toward the window, parted the drapes enough to squint through, and thought to myself, *Who in their right mind would actually build a hotel this close to a train track? And furthermore, who was that sweet, precious woman who arranged to have us stay here?* She said she lived in this neighborhood. Surely she knew about the trains that roared through at night. Though I wanted to be back asleep, I sort of couldn't wait for morning because when she came to pick us up, I had some things to talk with her about.

Finally we got settled again. Until 5:00, that is.

Before this third train had fully rattled by—laying hard on its horn, no less—Jerry and I just got on up. What's the use? Besides, I needed some time to rehearse my speech for the sweet little lady, who stopped by bright and early to welcome us to Saturday. Hardly had the "good mornings" gotten out of our mouths before I said, "Listen, let me ask you about this train that passed by last night"—to which she responded, "What train?"

Huh?

"Wait a minute," I answered, "you said you live in this neighborhood, didn't you? Did several trains not come through here last night—10:00, 1:00, 5:00?"

At this, she slapped her hand over her mouth, her eyes wide, her face fully apologetic. "Priscilla, Jerry," she said, "I totally forgot. We've lived in this neighborhood so long, and we've grown so accustomed to the sound of the trains, it doesn't even wake us up anymore. We don't even notice it."

*We don't even notice it . . .*

Something similar has happened in the "generational" neighborhood we call our own. With a church on every corner and a Christian radio station at nearly every point of the dial, with Christian bookstores in many shopping districts and more Bible resources available than ever, we've gotten so accustomed to the blessings of God, we've grown virtually deaf to His voice and blind to His presence. He's met us so frequently with what we need—everything from putting food on our table to keeping us from catching the flu—that we typically don't stop long enough to chalk up these daily benefits to His active care and provision.

But not only that, if He were to do something uniquely interesting in our lives, if He chose to display Himself outside His usual pattern, if the train of His glory were to come through in some remarkable way, is there a good chance we wouldn't even recognize it because we've lived in the neighborhood of His favor for so long?

May we not become desensitized to God's activity. May we stay keenly aware of the presence of God, even at night when the shadows are dim, even when listening for Him requires being able to pick out His gentle whisper in the silence, and even when we are walking through the in-between times. One-in-a-millions know that God has put them here—in this particular place, at this particular time—with certain things for them to experience. They're not afraid to live through the in-between, development times because the muscles they're growing out here in the wilderness are going to help them hit the Promised Land running. It's going to be worth it. They know it.

Oh Lord, make me a one-in-a-million!

## Playing Keep-Away

If we're not careful, our heart's descent into bitterness and complaining can be our undoing. One of the reasons the apostle Paul so sharply warned, "Do everything without complaining or arguing" (Phil. 2:14 NIV), was because he had seen those who had given themselves over to grumbling "and were destroyed by the destroyer" (1 Cor. 10:10). I know that complaining is what the in-between times seem to call for. But, my friend, the call toward discontentment leads you to places you never want to go, and it keeps you from seeing God's current blessings in your life. The spirit of complaint is born out of an unwillingness to trust God with today. Like the Israelites, it means you are spending your time looking back toward Egypt or wishing for the future, all the while missing what God is doing right now. If high blood pressure is the silent killer, a high bitterness quotient is its testy, evil brother. It takes what God is doing in your life and smashes it into a thousand wasted pieces.

And even in the in-between times, He *is* doing something.

That's why it is so important that you and I not see these as being dead zones. As I said before, they are more like bridges that take us from one point to another, always in the direction of where God is moving. If we can get it through our heads that this is not a waste of time or something to sleepwalk through, we can stand and celebrate the fact that God is active in our boredom. He is teaching great truth even in the midst of dry lecture.

You heard me right. In-between times are good times. When you spot one, relish it. Don't miss one moment of it. Sink in, and see the depths of God.

When we believe this with our whole hearts, it lets us in on one of the keys to successful, abundant living. Listen carefully now: the wilderness is not a barrier between us and abundant living. It may often feel like it, but it's not. The thing that barricades our entrance into Promised Land living is when we *wander* in the wilderness, when we delay our development process by refusing to stay near to God, even when He feels far away.

God obviously, as we have seen, led His people away from Egypt down a path that was far from easy and convenient. That's because nearness to Canaan was not His goal for this in-between time in their lives. The goal was nearness to *Him*. God chose the wilderness and all it would entail because He knew this was the best way to get them ready for what was to come—by drawing them closer to His side, teaching them to depend on Him for everything, helping them learn to follow even when their better judgment told them another path was preferable, certainly more pleasurable.

We are so convinced that the barren seasons of life are a departure from our main objectives. They seem to give us good reason for being angry with God for making us wait this long for what we want. Will we, you and especially me, ever get it through our heads that the wilderness is a *blessing* He gives to us in order that we might see Him more fully and completely, that we might love Him more intentionally and wholeheartedly? The wilderness is where we learn most clearly "that man does not live by bread alone, but man lives by everything that proceeds out of the mouth of the Lord" (Deut. 8:3).

Perhaps at this very moment the wilderness feels like it's draining you dry. The stinging winds and dusty conditions, the high heat and low visibility—they're only intensifying your desire for what you wish your life could be like right now. *What if? If only?* Those are the leading causes of spiritual stagnation on the road between here and abundance.

Will you trust God enough to believe that anywhere you can grow nearer to Him is the right place for you to be? The best approach to Canaan is not to go wandering around the wilderness, sure that you can find a better way to get out of here, grumbling and muttering as you go. The best way to Canaan is to walk straight through, wherever He leads, holding His invisible hand until you swear you can feel His pulse in your palm.

That's how close you are. That's how close He is.

## Glory, Glory

Readiness for Canaan.

Nearness to God.

These are healthy motivators to one-in-a-millions who keep their focus upward and their goals eternal. These are good reasons for getting up in the morning, even if breakfast is sure to be cooked on the in-between side. But of all the things to be looking and hoping for while we wait and wonder what's going to happen next, one objective tops them all.

Glory.

The Lord tipped His people off to this grand purpose for the wilderness when He announced, even as Pharaoh had set out with his troops to corral them at the Red Sea, "I will receive glory by means of Pharaoh and all his army, and the Egyptians will know that I am the LORD" (Exod. 14:4 HCSB).

Glory.

The Hebrew word for this is *kabed*, a term that means to be heavy, weighty, or burdensome.[13] It's the idea of a person's being fully believed and trusted, being given immense weight and credibility. This is what God was after, not only at the Red Sea but also in the days and years that followed—even in the in-between times, even in your time. He wants your life to give daily evidence of His presence as seen in the way you handle everything from prosperity to heartbreaking loss, everything from buzzed-up excitement to complete boredom. He wants His influence to weigh more heavily over your actions and decisions than all those me-first and people-pleasing attitudes that often come quickest to mind. He may even want you to be squeezed into a situation where no other explanation can suffice for your deliverance than that God has done something special for you.

Give Him glory.

I can look back at some of our past difficulties and dry patches and see the ways God eventually intervened to change things for the better. I remember the miracles He performed. I recall the unexpected convergence of events He caused to occur. I can still cite the details of how He performed a mighty rescue of our health, our finances, our prospects for the future. I can see (at least I *hope* I can see) how we gave Him glory for that—not perfectly but at least purposefully—and how anyone who either witnessed or heard of it should have been able to recognize it as the obvious work of God. I hope and pray that He grew in others' estimation as He threw His weight around in our lives and we did our best to point to Him as our Provider.

That's great. That's what's supposed to happen.

But here's how we test whether or not we're learning what God is teaching in His wilderness lectures. Here's how we know if we've been paying attention when He's made the circuit through our lives. If we have spiritual vision and anticipation to *expect* God to wring glory out of this in-between situation—a tight, uncomfortable spot that's a whole lot easier to gripe about than to pray over. (Now this—*this*—is what I've got to work on.) If we've grasped the fact that nearness to

God and a developing readiness for Canaan are more valuable than anything else. If we can keep ourselves fixated on reflecting His glory rather than repeating our self-consumed complaints.

What's He going to do to fix our situation? I don't know.

But what's going to happen if we yield to Him while we're in it? God's gettin' glory.

And I can live with that. How about you?

## In-Between Expectations

Our fathers in Egypt did not understand Your wonders; they did not remember Your abundant kindnesses, but rebelled by the sea, at the Red Sea. . . . They quickly forgot His works; they did not wait for His counsel . . . but grumbled in their tents; they did not listen to the voice of the LORD. (Ps. 106:7, 13, 25)

And what they missed as a result were numerous opportunities to recognize what God had done, what He was presently doing, and what He was still yet to do. God can and does move on behalf of His people. These thirsty in-between times when you are trudging through a particularly rough or stagnant patch have not fallen on you by mistake. He is making a way for His greatness to be seen, for His glory to be put on full display—a way for you to *experience* in real time what He promises to be when you're sitting on the pew, hoping it's true.

What are you asking God to do for you at this season of life? What would you say you most desire if you were able to verbalize it? What would be the most shocking, delightful outcome to whatever series of circumstances you're being called to walk through these days?

No, we can't demand that of God. He's not one who can be told what to do. But there's a world of difference between dictating and expecting. When we pray for what we most wish to happen, we can trust with absolute assurance that He will either act according to our prayer . . . or do something better. He will either bless us with what we want, or He'll bless us with what we really need and change our hearts to desire what He's given. He alone knows what will get us most prepared for our next stage of abundant living, what will draw us nearest to Him in fellowship and intimacy, what will cause His glory to burst upon the stage of our lives with weighty significance, where everybody who wants to can see it. We can totally rely on Him to take us exactly where we need to go . . . if we'll only be willing to follow.

You simply can't go wrong approaching an in-between time with that kind of heart and spirit. So be encouraged. You can stand in the midst of uncertainty, trusting that you are safe in your Father's arms. You can weather the slow and uneventful waiting, believing that He's taking you somewhere significant. You can endure the pain, even if it keeps you up at night. And you can experience a foretaste of glory even with a mouthful of bitter pills to swallow. Why? Because He's got more in store for you than you can ever imagine.

Be watching. Be waiting. Believe in between.

*I will lift up my eyes to the mountains; from where shall my help come? My help comes from the* LORD, *who made heaven and earth. He will not allow your foot to slip; He who keeps you will not slumber.*

PSALM 121:1–3

## CHAPTER 10

# Far and Near

MY FATHER AND MOTHER TOOK a number of mission trips when we were growing up. They might be gone a week or more on any one journey, and we'd miss them for (most of) the whole time. As the day grew close for their return, we were naturally excited to have them back home—assuming, of course, that they came bearing gifts.

It had become a family routine: (1) Parents leave. (2) They travel abroad. (3) They return with four shiny new trinkets, one for each of us.

Waiting anxiously inside the house on the day of their arrival, we'd hear their car pulling into the driveway, then bound out the back door in a four-headed bundle, almost flattening them with our enthusiastic welcome. I remember seeing my father's face light up with glee when he saw us, just before his expression dissolved into a disappointed frown as the first words out of our mouths were, "What'd you get me?" "What does it do?" "What does it say?" "Can I have it now?"

We didn't really want *them*. We just wanted what they'd brought us.

As I'm writing and remembering this, Jerry and I are on a flight home from London. In a matter of hours, we'll be back at the airport in Dallas. Our boys will be there, eager to see us . . . (won't they?). Or will we have to coerce a hug out of them as they lunge at our suitcases in search of what we've brought them?

Like mother, like sons, I guess.

Things really haven't changed much, have they? Yahweh Himself desired kids who would want *Him* more than they wanted the gifts He was able to give them. He sought to have intimacy with His people in order that they would long for the same thing in return. He hadn't freed them from Egypt merely to shower them with Promised Land gift packs, the latest from the milk-and-honey collection. He had brought them *out* so that He might bring them *unto* Himself. He had lifted them up "on eagles' wings" (Exod. 19:4) that He might settle them inside His loving, all-consuming presence. It's what some have described as the "heart of the Old Testament,"[14] this passage in Exodus 19 that reflects the sheer depths of fellowship and relationship that God desired with His people. This was why He had led them out on pilgrimage in the first place—to develop in them a heart of passion for Himself. This was why He had led them this far.

And "far" was the right word for it.

Three months of long, hot travel had positioned them deep in the wilderness of Sinai, down near the southernmost tip of its rugged peninsula, close to where it dipped into the sea. This part of the journey would be the farthest point of their travel away from the Promised Land. In this place they most likely felt the most lost, the most desperate, the most frustrated, and the most disappointed since leaving Egypt.

I can hear God's people asking, "God, do You know where we are?"

How I wish they could hear—how I wish *we* could hear—His assuring response, "Ahh, yes. I certainly do."

For dominating the landscape in this area was a mountain—one that carried great significance, a fact they would soon become awesomely aware of—a mountain so holy that it was known by its own special, quite characteristic name: "the mountain of God" (Exod. 3:1; 24:13). This was no random map feature. It would be the focal point of the Hebrews' attention for the next eleven months. It would witness the zenith of the entire book of Exodus. It was here that God planned to cement the relationship He had been developing in them for the past many weeks. And this is where He would extend to them a divine invitation they'd hopefully not refuse.

> The LORD said to Moses, "Behold, I will come to you in a thick cloud, so that the people may *hear* when I speak . . . and let them be ready for the third day, for on the third day the LORD will come down on Mount Sinai *in the sight of all the people.*" (Exod. 19:9, 11, author italics)

There it was. Like a gold-sealed love letter floating down to Earth from the heavens, beckoning them to new heights of intimacy. Yahweh summoned His people to hear Him and see Him for themselves. For the first time they were receiving an opportunity to do something they'd never done before. Yes, they had been following Him from the very day they were delivered out of Egypt. They had seen His miraculous provision here and there along the way, and they had heard His word delivered through their leader, Moses. But now they had a chance to *hear* God's voice with their own ears, to *see* the outward manifestation of His glory with their own eyes. And this chance came, this opportunity was offered, this invitation was given in this wilderness. At Sinai.

Oh, Sinai.

So far, and yet so close . . . close to God, that is. While divine intimacy would occur in this place, there was a great distance between its geographical location and the Promised Land. While scholars debate the exact number of miles between the two, it is clear that this stop on their journey put them at the farthest distance from their desired destination.

While so much of what Canaan represented to Israel and to its neighbors was a life of *external* blessing and abundance, Sinai represented a place of *internal* blessing and abundance. And the two were nowhere near each other. Maybe Yahweh knew that the blessings of Canaan might blind His people to the priority of relationship with Him. So He led them in the opposite direction first to secure their loyalty. And when their journey led them far away from the possible distraction of milk and honey, they came face-to-face with God. It wasn't until they had been allowed to sink to their lowest ebb that they were ready to be called into full commitment to Him, established as His chosen people, and invited into covenant relationship.

Are you at Sinai today? Are you at a station in life that seems to you (or to others, as they peer inside) as though it is the total opposite of blessing and fulfillment? Then let Sinai remind you not to be discouraged. God has brought you to this place, for in it stands a mountain in which God's presence will appear. Often when external blessing seems to elude us, internal spiritual gifts come tumbling our direction. Sometimes—not always but sometimes—it takes being in the worst shape of your life to see and hear the Lord.

Maybe that's why the Sinai experience—the opportunity to meet Yahweh in a fresh way—didn't come until three months to the day after the Israelites had left Egypt. "On that very day" (Exod. 19:1)—and not one day too soon—God brought them to Sinai. They were fresh on the heels of a tense battle with the Amalekites, the one where Aaron and Hur had to hold up Moses' weary arms in order for the people to prevail. In these past months they'd not only met enemies; they'd also trod the hot, dusty terrain of the wilderness on foot, run for their lives from Pharaoh, and suffered hunger and extreme thirst. Perhaps it was only after allowing three months of wilderness hardship that they were ready for what God was about to give.

Wading through a time of difficulty under His protective guidance often prepares our hearts to accept His invitation and become ready to walk with Him in a covenantal relationship. Sometimes it's only after undergoing the fight of our lives that our desire to meet Him on the mountain comes into full bloom.

So the timing of the Israelites' arrival in Sinai was not accidental. Being in this place on this day was carefully calculated by God. The timing and the circumstances surrounding it were of paramount importance to completing the work God wanted to do in the hearts of His people before He led them into the land of promise.

Hear that again for yourself: being in *this place*—"on this very day"—is not accidental. It is His perfect timing that has brought you to this point in your journey and to His mountain with a tender heart, ready to receive His invitation to nearness.

It had to be here. It had to be now. This was God's chosen time and place. The great work God wants to do in our hearts—obtaining intimacy and fellowship with the Lover of our souls, refining our passions, and steering them toward Himself—often happens at the farthest possible point from where we think our greatest blessings are coming from. It happens at Sinai.

This book is in your hand right now, and you are scouring this chapter with your eyes at this moment because God is inviting you to turn your eyes to the mountain. Look up, my friend! Sinai is before you.

## Drawn from a Distance

Jordan was six years old when he suffered his first seizure. He was a bright, rambunctious boy whose body had never given him or anyone else the first indication that something was amiss. Up until then, he had been basically the picture of health. That's what made this all so sudden. Shocking.

You can imagine how frightened he was. You can imagine, too, how distressed his parents were, especially when doctors revealed the source of the problem. Jordan had a brain tumor. To make matters worse, the mass was located in a region of the brain that made it inoperable. Even trying to perform a biopsy to confirm whether it was cancerous or not was deemed too risky. Left with few options, Jordan's mom and dad were sent home with medications to give him, hoping these would help stop or at least minimize the threat of future episodes.

Yet the seizures persisted. And each time he experienced one, his memory was noticeably affected. He began to lose words from his memory bank, being forced to piece together his own form of sign language to compensate for the deficiency. This was bad and getting worse.

You might say they felt as far away from Canaan as they could possibly get.

Oh, how they begged God for a miracle, as any of us would. How they begged Him for answers. They lay awake at night, wondering why God would allow their precious son to be afflicted like this, why anyone so young would have to become this familiar with doctors and hospitals and difficult conversations. How could God possibly get glory from something that was proving so debilitating and seemingly irreversible?

I'll go ahead and tell you that, in time, God provided a surgeon who was able to operate and remove Jordan's tumor. He's now a healthy young man with few traces of the harrowing illness he once suffered. But his mom, reflecting on what they went through in the darkest of those days, had this to say:

This experience was required so I could lay down my independence on myself and depend on God. I have indeed learned to trust God for *everything* in my life. I fooled myself into thinking that before all this I had given my whole life to God and looked to Him for every answer. What I learned through this season of life was, that simply wasn't true. I may have *desired* to give it all to Him, but in the back of my mind, I held on to the things I thought I could take care of.

Once Jordan's tumor began to grow and it was determined that he would need to undergo the surgery, I had no choice but to let go and let God have His way. I certainly couldn't go to college and get a degree in neurosurgery in six months, so I had to trust God to take care of Jordan. And I knew He would—no matter the outcome. God knows what will happen in my life, and He has a plan for me that's better than anything I could map out for myself.

That's a woman who's quit seeking God's treats. He had taken her as far away from her hoped-for destination as she'd ever dreamed possible. He had positioned her in Sinai, miles and miles from everything she thought abundant life was supposed to taste and feel like. But in this place she'd met Him in a new way. She had seen His face. She had heard His voice. In fact, Promised Land living had already begun for her because now only one thing mattered anymore: she just wanted God, not just His gifts.

And though our circumstances may be entirely different from hers, this is the turn that all our journeys must take—toward a mountain of experience with God that marks us as His people forever, that draws us into fellowship like never before.

The dry, dusty wilderness is always designed to lead us to Sinai.

## From the Bottom Looking Up

Every wilderness journey has a Sinai experience. In fact, I believe it's the primary purpose for God's leading us this way. And like the one the Israelites encountered, ours will likely occur when we find ourselves far, far away from the Promised Land. I'm not saying that we're *required* to hit rock bottom before being able to enjoy true intimacy with God. But it is often when we're at our lowest point—financially, relationally, professionally, physically, emotionally, or even spiritually—that God ignites our hearts in a whole new way. It's when we find the journey getting tougher than we'd ever imagined it could be that we should look up in expectation of an experience, an invitation from God we've not had before.

If you're familiar with me at all, you know my testimony of being in a relationship during college that I was certain would lead to marriage. When it all fell apart, the weight of the rejection just devastated me to the point of threatening my emotional and physical health.

How well I remember the day I reached my lowest point. I was driving down Highway 75 in Dallas, crying a river of tears—crying so hard, in fact, that I could barely see the road in front of me. Realizing I could no longer drive safely from the sobbing, I pulled the car to the shoulder and buried my face in my hands. My heart ached. My spirit was broken. I begged God aloud to please—*please*—restore this relationship that I longed for so desperately.

And in my extreme distress the Holy Spirit communicated to me this unforgettable thought: "He doesn't want you, Priscilla, and you still want a relationship with him. I *do* want you. Why don't you just have a relationship with Me?"

At that moment I lifted my head and, through my tears, I saw the mountain of God. My gold-sealed invitation came, calling me into a more intimate relationship with Him.

I sat there by the side of the road, my emotions in tatters, feeling like I was as far away from Canaan as I'd ever been. Yet this level of devastation, this level of brokenness, had my heart sensitive enough to recognize and engage in what God wanted to do in my life. As He said of His people through the prophet Hosea, "When they finally hit rock bottom, maybe they'll come looking for me" (Hosea 5:15 *The Message*).

Maybe?

Yes, only maybe.

Being at Sinai can cause a backlash, you know. Left to our own devices, our frustration and disappointment can easily cause us to turn our backs on the mountain of God instead of facing it full on. We can become so impatient with the day-to-day, mundane circumstances filling our lives that we keep our heads down instead of turning them up toward the peak of His presence. Maybe, just maybe, we can miss the invitation and our opportunity, while sitting in a far-from-Canaan point, to encounter God in a way that will revolutionize our lives.

Lord, have mercy. Don't let us miss it.

## Campground Stories

I know how you feel. You want to get out of the wilderness and away from the Sinai Peninsula as quickly as you can, right? You're praying that the season of life you're journeying through right now will come to a close before this book does. But what if you hurry through it only to realize later that you missed it—that you missed *Him?* What if there were things God wanted to show you, experiences with Himself that He wanted to give you, but you rushed right past in your haste to get out of town?

Israel, led by a man who knew a thing or two about meeting God in the wilderness, chose to handle Sinai differently than I normally do. Moses, you see, had been here before. He was no stranger to this place, remember, or to rock bottom. He'd been to Horeb before (another name for Sinai). At forty years of age, he had run for his life from Pharaoh's palace. Once the prince of Egypt, he had forfeited his rights to the throne by killing an Egyptian soldier he'd seen abusing one of his fellow Hebrews. When Pharaoh discovered what Moses had done, he sought to kill him, and Moses fled into the wilderness.

You know what happened next. "During that long period" (Exod. 2:23 NIV), he poked and prodded his new father-in-law's flocks along the foothills of this mountain until the day God drew his eye to a burning bush and an encounter with the eternal I AM. During this most unsure, most uncomfortable season of his life, Moses had been supernaturally swept up into intimacy with God, his life's mission altered from that day forward. If anybody knew how a Sinai experience could change a life and modify the existence of a whole nation, it was Moses. So when he approached the mountain of God for a second time, leading a human flock instead of a four-legged one, he fully expected to "see and hear." No doubt, he was brimming with a holy anticipation.

And so under His leadership, "Israel camped in front of the mountain" (Exod. 19:2). And there they stayed. For eleven more months.

The meaning of the original word for "camped" in Exodus 19:2 means to pitch a tent, to dwell, to rest. It was always a temporary protective enclosure for a tribe, never a permanent one. Get this image in your mind: two million refugees unpacking their knapsacks, pitching their tents, and corralling their livestock for an extended stay. This must have been quite an effort, a frustrating one at that. This wasn't their ultimate destination, and they knew it. This wasn't what they had left Egypt to find, and yet under the covering of God's guiding cloud, they chose to open the divine invitation. They decided to settle in, pitch their tent, camp out—questions and all—and turn their attention to God's mountain.

I know when I'm in the wilderness of uncertainty, with all those piercing "why" and "how" questions hanging over my head, the last thing I want to do is to pitch my tent and just camp out awhile. I don't want to settle in and get comfortable with this part of the journey. When I'm in a season of life that I don't want to be in, it's hard for me to unpack my bags and trust God to move me when it's an appropriate time. My first inclination is to escape the shadow of God's guidance, to run out ahead of Him, to get out of here as soon as possible.

But ancient Israel teaches us differently. It seems they knew that camping out in their curved formation around the mountain would not only allow them the privilege of beholding God on this leg of the journey, but it would also be a protective enclosure for them while they were here. Their formation was strategic and would assist in warding off any enemies that may have tried to invade. Being at this mountain, settled under the shadow of God's presence, was far better than being in a different, albeit more comfortable place without His presence nearby. The same is true for you and me, you know. You are better protected in the wilderness at Sinai with God than someplace else without Him.

So Israel didn't hurry onward, passing up God's guiding cloud in an effort to move on with their journey. Even with an unsettled future and millions of questions swimming in their minds, not totally clear as to why God would bring them to this place, they stopped and camped. They watched and listened. And they were not disappointed. "The LORD came down on Mount Sinai, to the top of the mountain" (Exod. 19:20).

Aah. God came down. And Israel beheld Him.

Allow me to offer you the same encouragement that Moses undoubtedly extended to the people before climbing up to receive God's law and commandments: *camp here at the mountain.* When you find that you're at the end of yourself, when it seems the gap between you and your destiny is more vast than it's ever been, look up so you don't miss God coming down. An invitation is on the way with your name on it. It's an opportunity for you to have an experience with God that will change your walk with Him forever. Stay engaged in what He wants to accomplish in this important season of learning and relationship building. Don't be afraid to make your home here at the mountain of God for as long as it takes before the cloud of His presence declares the road safe for travel again. Don't rush the wilderness, and don't rush the Sinai experience.

Wait.

Sit tight.

Give it time.

Chill.

Unpack your bags. Because camping out is part of this journey. Patience is part of what's required for our hearts to get in tune with God's desires.

Want the Giver, not just His gifts. Don't head out until you've seen and heard the Lord.

Despite the difficulty of your journey, despite all the questions you've brought with you, despite all the discomfort and impatience you may be feeling, I urge you to engage fully in every season you get to spend at Sinai. Don't leave your bags packed and keep working out of your travel kit. Don't sleep with your clothes on or put the moving company on speed-dial. Don't miss out on what God wants to do with you "this very day," even at the furthest point from your hopes and dreams. Your meeting with Him in this wilderness has been planned for this moment. Look and listen.

As it turns out, this high point on the Israelites' wilderness journey is symbolic of the high point in our lives as well. This is the reason He saved you, lifted you up, and chose to bring you close.

So nail your tent pegs deep. And turn your eyes to the mountain.

*[He] is a God who is jealous about his relationship with you.*

EXODUS 34:14 NLT

CHAPTER 11

# Wholly His

JACKSON WAS ONLY FOUR MONTHS old, traveling with us by plane for the first time. I had fallen asleep while Jerry sat holding him in the seat next to mine. Suddenly a foul odor jarred me awake. I turned to Jerry, who was still holding Jackson but was no longer holding him close. A contorted expression on his face, my husband now held his beloved firstborn son with outstretched arms.

Mama to the rescue.

I grabbed a diaper and some baby powder from our carry-on bag and hustled Jackson to the airplane bathroom, expecting a routine clean-and-change operation. Not so. It turned out to be full-on damage control. Toxic waste removal.

I can honestly say I'd never seen anything quite like this. I'll spare you the worst of the details, but suffice to say, a full bath was required, and all of his clothes were thrown away. When I finally emerged from the tiny lavatory, I felt really bad for the unsuspecting stranger who would have to enter next.

Returning to my seat, I handed Jackson back to his father. We shared a wordless glance that communicated the severity of the blow-out, as well as the restoration of clean living conditions. Jerry smiled, looked into the dreamy eyes of his freshly bathed, sweet-smelling infant, and cradled him closely to his chest for the remainder of the ride home. While their relationship as father and son had never changed, the level of intimacy between them had been momentarily interrupted.

Moments earlier the child had needed to be held at arm's length. Now he was in intimate relationship with his father.

Like Jerry with his son, our heavenly Father desires to hold us close. There's nothing that can change your Father-child relationship, but intimacy is the passion of God—His most zealous pursuit. And yet this closeness is utterly unattainable until the filthy stench and stain of our sin has been removed and eliminated. If we ever desire to go from arm's length to cradled nearness in our relationship with God, we're going to need changing. Big time.

But that's one of the things a Sinai experience is designed to accomplish—bringing us face-to-face with God's call to personal holiness. When we truly begin to desire Him more than we desire the land to which He is taking us, we don't want anything to stand in the way of intimacy. When we truly begin to understand God's loving heart toward us and when we internalize the lengths to which He has gone to have relationship with us, we start to feel differently when His Word and His Spirit demand our obedience.

Just consider the amazing feats He has pulled off to establish relationship with us—how He has delivered us from our slavery to sin, how He has sustained us and drawn us to Himself (Exod. 19:4). Knowing that we are loved like this should cause us to want to love Him back. With this on our minds, no longer does denying our sin and doing what He requires seem frustrating and burdensome, unattainable and overwhelming. Rather, following Him with our whole heart becomes a joy. It's what we want because we understand that being near Him is more than worthwhile. The benefits of Promised Land living are an automatic outcome of a deep love relationship. Being near Him now is worth any expense, any so-called sacrifice. It's as though we've been given a "new heart" and a "new spirit"—the removal of our "heart of stone," replaced by a "heart of flesh" (Ezek. 36:26)—the better to love Him.

And so He called Israel to holiness at Sinai, just as He calls us to holiness today—not to keep us from having fun but to allow us the intimacy that will give us the milk-and-honey living we've been longing for.

This message of required holiness was the first one that God gave to His chosen people as they stood at the mountain of God.

> Now then, if you will indeed obey My voice and keep My
> covenant, then you shall be My own possession among all
> the peoples, for all the earth is Mine; and you shall be to Me a
> kingdom of priests and a holy nation. (Exod. 19:5–6)

Before we can begin to contemplate this clear call to obedient living, we must remember this appeal for the people to "obey" His voice came three months into their journey—only *after* their deliverance from Egypt—just as His appeal to us comes *after* we have received His forgiveness for our sins by placing faith in Christ and being delivered from our own slavery. Holiness was not a requirement for their deliverance. That had already been given. The call to live holy came *after* they'd been made free by the One who loved them most.

No one is expected to be good enough to earn salvation. No one. No amount of holy living can earn you a spot in eternity. But after we have received the grace of God, we are given the Holy Spirit to indwell us. Then, and only then, are we empowered to become people who actually have the capability of doing and thinking righteous things. As a result we have the opportunity to share in the same benefit package He was extending for the first time to His people, Israel, including the privilege of living with the following identities:

- Being His "own possession"—every person highly valued by and related to Him (Exod. 19:5).
- "A kingdom of priests"—each individual having full access to Him, with the nation as a whole acting as priests to promote the knowledge of God and to mediate His blessings to the nations of the world (Exod. 19:6).
- "A holy nation"—set apart for His service and purposes (Exod. 19:6).

In this Sinai experience God was in the process of drawing His people closer than ever. He inspired them to live in conformity with what He was teaching and revealing to them so they could receive the benefits of all that their relationship should entail. And just so they'd know the benefits they would receive and have assurance that their obedience would be worth their while, He offered them the same thing He offers us—a covenant.

## Promised Nearness

All covenants are initiated by God. The term "covenant" in the original Hebrew language is *berith,* a promise or an agreement between God and man.[15] Therefore, even a covenant like the one offered at Sinai, a *conditional* covenant based on the people's obedience, is still a pure act of God's grace and kindness toward fallen individuals who don't deserve a single divine glance. The Scripture contains several examples of conditional covenants between God and His people. His covenant with Adam, for example, contained a condition that he not eat "from the tree of the knowledge of good and evil" (Gen. 2:17). But His covenant with Abraham—"I will make you a great nation, and I will bless you, and make your name great" (Gen. 12:2)—was not dependent at all on Abraham's commitment to follow through. Instead it was completely dependent on God's unwavering steadfastness. The fact that God had chosen Israel, freed them from bondage, and sustained them throughout their long journey in the wilderness—despite their grumbling and complaining—was a direct result of God's unconditional covenant with their forefather Abraham.

Yet the time had come for the children of Israel no longer to ride the coattails of those who had gone before. God deemed it necessary at this moment in His people's history, at this profound Sinai experience, that they make their own personal commitment to Him. So He reached out to them by way of an "if/then" conditional covenant. In order to receive the benefits that Yahweh was offering, the people would have to "obey" His voice and "keep" His covenant. The sheer joy of knowing Him, being near Him, and remembering all He had done for them were to be their ongoing motivations for following Him. And *if* they obeyed, *then* they would receive the benefits of the covenant.

Today you and I still interact with God on the basis of covenant—except that as a believer in Christ and as a member of His church, we have been given an *unconditional* promise of permanent standing before our holy God. The New Testament mirror of the Mosaic covenant reveals that the benefit package, which extended to the early Hebrews, based on their obedience, is ours without condition, based on the righteousness of Christ.

> You are a chosen race, a royal priesthood, a holy nation, a
> people for God's own possession, so that you may proclaim the
> excellencies of Him who has called you out of darkness into His
> marvelous light. (1 Pet. 2:9)

No strings attached. No work required. It's all grace, all the time.

It brings tears to my eyes, really, this unabandoned love extended to the church by a holy God. I'm stunned and in complete awe that He knows my weaknesses and shortcomings. He has complete fore-knowledge of my future failures, and yet He offers me so much abundance—without condition! Shouldn't the knowledge that God has given us gifts with no strings attached cause us to want to love Him more, depend on Him more fully, and obey Him more completely? If Israel was compelled to obey (see Exod. 19:8) on the basis of a conditional covenant, how much more should the church feel compelled today?

Let your time camped out in the foothills of Sinai remind you of the unconditional standing of righteousness you've been given by God *despite* the fact that we don't always keep our side of the bargain.

So what do we do when we aren't experiencing the benefits of the covenant we know we've been given? Who or what is the culprit when we are not *experiencing* our tremendous value to God, not *experiencing* the kind of nearness a child feels for the father who loves her, not *experiencing* how it feels to know that our lives are lining up with the purposes God has for us as His "chosen race," His "royal priesthood," His "holy nation," a people called to be His "own possession"? A quick look in the mirror of Isaiah 59:2 might help us with the answer: "But your iniquities have made a separation between you and your God, and your sins have hidden His face from you so that He does not hear."

Who's the culprit? You.

What's the problem? Sin.

We hold ourselves at arm's length from the One who made us, redeemed us, and longs to hold us close. Our negligence or rebellion against His grace results in a sense of distance. We forfeit nearness for . . . nothing. With reasonings that run from outright sinister to just plain silly, we toy with sin and rebellion and play around with its consequences. And while we are no longer under the law, not needing to strive in order to win God's acceptance, we must take seriously His call to holy, daily living if we want the kind of fellowship that results in life-altering encounters with God.

What has He asked you to do—I mean, just in the last twenty-four hours? Are you doing it? Are you being obedient to what He's said? Or are you avoiding His instructions, maybe just delaying your obedience? Whether or not you comply could mean the difference between sitting across the table from Him or sitting in His lap. Is it worth it?

Not to Him.

Not with all the milk and honey He so desperately wants to give.

So sometimes when we fall short, our tenacious, pursuing God—unwilling to leave us dangling at arm's length—leads us by His well-disguised mercy to Sinai, where we come face-to-face with who He is and what He's done, where we realize again that there's no substitute for seeing personal holiness become the actual way our average day plays out. By submitting ourselves to God's desires for our lives, letting the holiness He has ascribed to us through Christ become the holiness He grows in us on a regular basis, we feel our head being cushioned against His breast. We experience in our mind, body, and emotions what He has already made a reality by virtue of His redeeming grace.

We're drawn close. And in ways that our sin has attempted to steal from us, we feel at home again. Right where our God wants us to be.

## Lost and Found

We took our boys to Disney World a few years ago. And we had a "magical" time, for the most part. But one particular part of our experience in the Magic Kingdom was far from enchanting.

If you've been there, you know that one of the areas in the park includes an enormous playground for the toddlers (or perhaps actually for the parents, who need a place to sit down and catch their breath). While Jerry went to find us something to eat, I sat and watched our three-year-old Jackson going up and down the slide, walking across the balance beam, weaving in and out of the tunnels. It wasn't long, however, before his little one-year-old brother was begging—in his one-year-old way—to join the fun.

What does Mama do in a situation like that? She can't very well turn her baby loose to get trampled by squealing Disney toddlers. So Mama did what mamas do. Tucking my little one in my arms, I climbed up on the ladder, teetered him across the walking platforms, even swooshed down the twisty slide with him held tightly in front of me. He was giggling hard by the time we reached bottom, and I let him drop to his own feet, as though he had done it himself. I dusted him off, smiles and all, and turned around to see if his big brother was maybe trailing close behind.

"Jackson?" Couldn't see him.

"Jackson?" Not up, not down, not crawling in the back.

"JACKSON?"

I asked the other mothers who were seated nearby if they'd seen a little African-American boy, about this tall, red T-shirt, Mickey Mouse ears.

No. Maybe.

Everywhere I looked, I saw children. But no Jackson. And in those frantic few moments when a mother knows her child is missing but doesn't know where to look for him—and starts thinking the absolute worst—I began begging God as I never had before, "Please bring me back my boy!" Crying, searching, desperate, I hunted my Jackson this way and that, joined by Magic Kingdom staffers who suddenly appeared out of nowhere, asking me questions, helping me look. Finally after fifteen of the longest minutes I've ever endured in my life, I spotted a Disney World attendant walking toward me, holding little Jackson by the hand. Apparently he had come off the jungle gym soon after I had gotten up to take his little brother in, and he had gone out to look for me.

I ran to him and clutched him in my arms. We found a nearby place to sit down, and I cuddled my two boys close to me, one on each side, while I was still crying and thanking God that my children were safe and right here with me.

And in that moment of precious relief, even as Disney noise and music played all around us, I sensed the Holy Spirit speaking to me, saying, "Priscilla, you couldn't take fifteen minutes separated from your son. How do you think I felt when I willingly gave up my Boy for you, when I sat in the heavens and watched Him being tortured for you? That's how crazy I am about you."

What a great sacrifice it was!

Yes, our God, in His covenant love for us, has made a way for us to be held close in His passionate embrace through the saving blood of Jesus Christ. How foolish of us then, after receiving such boundless mercy, after seeing evidence of His provision everywhere we look, to resist His beckoning call to "draw near," knowing by His promise that He will draw near to us (James 4:8).

Yet this is what we often do. As American philosopher Sam Pascoe has observed, "Christianity began in Palestine as a fellowship (a relationship), and then moved on to Greece and became a philosophy (a way to think). Afterward it moved on to Rome and became an institution (a place to go), and then to Europe where it became a culture (a way of life). Finally it settled in America, where it has become an enterprise (a business)."[16] Our tendency over time is to maintain a comfortable distance between ourselves and God, keeping Him where we can manage Him, exchanging intimacy for ritual, afraid that closeness will also mean a loss of freedom.

But stop resisting what God is doing here at Sinai. Relinquish anything that keeps you consistently pulling away. Rest in His nearness. Hear Him—experience Him—drawing you closer.

## Obedience, Then Experience

Israel's experience at Sinai shows us a pattern that is worth taking note of. Their experience in hearing and seeing God didn't come until after "the people answered together and said, 'All that the LORD has spoken we will do!'" (Exod. 19:8). On the heels of their commitment to obedience on this mountain, the mountain of God at Sinai, His people heard Him with confidence for the first time.

I don't guess I know any believer who's not interested in hearing from God. But I know plenty, including me sometimes, who don't want their faith and obedience to be required in the process. We want to hear from God without wanting God. We want to receive His direction without *following* His directions, without taking time to know His heart by participating in holiness, which the Bible says is "the beauty of Your house" (Ps. 93:5 HCSB). But the fact is, living uprightly is a prerequisite for Promised Land living. Being aware of His presence, hearing His voice, and experiencing His power are contingent upon our submission to Him as Lord. "To him who orders his way aright I shall show the salvation of God" (Ps. 50:23). Choosing obedience even before we see its benefits will always pay off.

Obedience. Then experience.

Most often they still work in that order.

We serve a God who desires to be heard. In fact, as we've been discovering throughout our journey together, He will often allow us to embark on a wilderness experience so that our spiritual ears are more fully open to what He has to say.

Whether or not the people actually heard the audible voice of God at Sinai is a matter of theological debate, although He clearly stated in Exodus 19:9 that He would communicate with Moses in such a way that "the people may hear when I speak with you." Nonetheless, I don't think the difference of scholarly opinion is the point of this text. The fact is, they *heard* Him, and that's all that mattered.

I've never heard God speak in a voice I could hear with my ears. I've never known or met anyone who has. But look at the lengths He went to get His people to this place where they could hear what He had to say. And if you find yourself in a wilderness season in your own life, you can be sure that He will go through equally astounding lengths to reveal Himself to you. Know with full confidence that your heart is being prepared even now for the Spirit's personal guidance.

Often God's voice becomes louder for me in the wilderness of uncertainty—the times when my heart is the most tender and my spirit the most sensitive. That's when He pulls out His megaphone to give me a message I absolutely know is from Him. It may not be the fill-in-the-blank answer to my most burning questions. But there is often just an awareness of His presence that I've not known before. As a result I emerge from these wilderness periods with a more confident, comprehensive ability to discern His leading.

## The Balancing Act

So God wants us close. He wants intimacy and fellowship. He wants friendship. Exodus 19 and the original Sinai experience established that beyond any doubt. This desire for closeness reveals His *immanence,* His presence and sustaining involvement in our lives. And yet just a few verses away, we get a clear view of the majesty and holiness of the same God who wants to draw us near. This is His *transcendence*—His otherness, being above and separate from us.

When God met with Moses at Sinai, He said to His servant: "Go to the people and consecrate them today and tomorrow, and let them wash their garments; and let them be ready for the third day, for on the third day the LORD will come down on Mount Sinai in the sight of all the people. . . But do not let the priests and the people breakthrough to come up to the LORD lest He break forth upon them" (Exod. 19:10–11, 24).

He had invited them to intimacy, yes. But now, before giving them the Ten Commandments to which they would be held accountable, He brought a fitting balance to their relationship. This outward action of washing their clothes—complete enough to require three full days to achieve—was symbolic of the cleansing that should have been taking place in their hearts. The boundaries He set up around the mountain, punishable by death if violated, were another reminder that He would not be treated with casual indifference. Although immanence was His priority, He would not sacrifice His transcendence on its altar.

He was not to be taken lightly. He was not their buddy. He was God. He *is* God! And we cannot expect to hear and see Him if we remain resistant in conforming our lives to His lordship, His Word, and His character. If it takes a wilderness to help us understand, He is immanent enough to engage Himself that personally in our lives. And knowing that we need even more, He is transcendent enough to accomplish through this wilderness season what no human could (or would) ever do alone.

And so in one single chapter of the Bible, we see two very real, very important sides of the same God. This remains one of the rare blessings of our Sinai experiences, even today. They help us keep these two ongoing realities of God in healthy balance.

Throughout the history of the church, God's people have tended to swing from one of these two emphases to the other. During the days when sprawling cathedrals were built to honor the holiness and awesomeness of God, a tighter focus on His transcendence often kept Christians from personalizing their relationship with Him or from believing that they could experience intimate fellowship. During other seasons when the church has put more of an accent on His immanence, believers have emphasized relationship to the exclusion of appropriate fear and awe. Treating Him more like a friend than a holy God leads us to overlook the fact that He is intolerant of rebellion, that He is characterized by His wrath and justice as much as by His mercy and grace.

If we lean toward one or the other of these attributes of God in our modern culture, it is probably away from His transcendence. I don't say this because our churches are becoming more casual and laid-back or our worship styles more contemporary. I say it because we have a careless commitment to church attendance and don't give adequate priority to being active in ministry. I say it because we have a lazy approach to spending time with God and are not careful to remain obedient to Him. The attitudes and behaviors of too many believers today are not much different from the ones we see and expect of men and women who have no fear of God at all.

Oh, may our hearts never forget what we see and experience at Sinai, what we hear and feel when God gets our full attention and we behold His splendor. The vastness of His transcendence will shatter the thin security of our own self-righteousness, and a clear view of His holiness will drive us to our knees in repentance. We need these two aspects of God to remain in a holy tension, both calling us to obedience and calling us near in one sweeping motion.

A revelation of His majesty is not designed to scare us any more than it was meant to cause ancient Israel to run in fear of Him. When they saw the smoke and fire and heard the trumpet and all that thunder, they weren't supposed to shake in their boots and run for cover. The word Moses used in Exodus 20:20, in telling the people not to be "afraid" of the transcendence of God carries the idea of not being terrified or paralyzed by fear. But the fear He called them to balance in their lives was a fearful reverence that inspires humility, worship, and obedience. "God has come in order to test you," he said, "and in order that the fear of Him may remain with you, so that you may not sin" (Exod. 20:20)—so that you may then experience His nearness, so that you can know His immanence and transcendence in balanced harmony. God didn't display His glory on the mountain so that they would run *from* Him but rather run *to* Him.

There's just no escaping the holiness of God and His holy requirement of us—not for salvation but definitely for advancing beyond pew-sitting indifference, the kind that moves into pavement-walking freedom.

So here we stand with the children of Israel, our feet perhaps planted in places we don't really want them to be, camping out in a location we'd just as soon be seeing in our rearview mirror. I understand your frustration. I've been there. I've felt it. I understand your weariness. I've known days when I didn't see how I could possibly make it through, just as you have.

But my friend, please don't waste what God is developing in you out here in the wilderness. Don't prepare to leave Sinai until living a fully committed, fully expectant life with Christ is what you want more than anything. Press into Him. Camp at the mountain. Look up and see Him in all His splendor and glory. Be astounded again at His goodness, His power, and His holiness. The more clearly He comes into view, the more fully humbled and in awe of Him you will become.

He has made a way in the wilderness that will lead you toward your destiny. And as you approach it, as you begin living it, you'll look down and see a more complete person than you brought with you from Egypt. More grounded. More grateful. Less insistent. Less demanding. More patient. More confident in His all-sufficient sovereignty.

More wholly His.

# Part Three

# Destiny

*Do you see what this means—all these pioneers who blazed the way, all these veterans cheering us on? It means we'd better get on with it. Strip down, start running—and never quit! No extra spiritual fat, no parasitic sins. Keep your eyes on Jesus, who both began and finished this race we're in. Study how he did it. Because he never lost sight of where he was headed— that exhilarating finish in and with God—he could put up with anything along the way: cross, shame, whatever. And now he's there, in the place of honor, right alongside God.*

HEBREWS 12:1–2 THE MESSAGE

CHAPTER 12

# Winds of Change

THE CRUISING SPEED OF AN average 1940s airplane was around 200 miles per hour. So when aerospace companies began tinkering with new designs, hoping to achieve higher speeds, it seemed like insanity to consider building a jet that could approach the speed of sound—761 miles per hour. But that became the impossible goal. And by designing an aircraft that was more rocket than plane, and tapping a young aviator who was more daredevil than most, the dream of breaking the sound barrier became reality on October 14, 1947, when Chuck Yeager flew at supersonic speeds for nearly twenty seconds.

It could never have been enough just to *think* about flying faster than any human had ever traveled before or simply to draw blueprints and make calculations. The only way to break this unknown, uncharted barrier was for someone to be willing to do things differently than they'd always been done—to climb into the cockpit, activate the engines, and blast ahead with all the courage and determination a person can muster. That's the difference between a life that goes bust and a life that goes *boom!*

The journey through and out of the wilderness—the journey of life with Christ—is all about breaking barriers. It's about choosing to be someone who goes all-in with God, unlike the countless others who sit at home and watch their destiny go by. While millions live somewhere between pessimism and plain ordinary, expecting little of themselves and even less of God, the "one-in-a-millions" refuse to let their lives be defined by normal limitations and mundane routines. Most people let the barriers win. A few—those willing to do things differently—crash through and enter in. Why shouldn't that someone be you?

You probably know that when a jet plane flies faster than the speed of sound, it creates a loud popping sound that can be heard for miles around. What's not as commonly known is that at certain altitudes and in certain conditions, a white cloud of condensation can also be seen surrounding the plane at the moment it reaches the precise velocity. So this is more than just an aeronautic event; it's a happening that draws other people into the experience. They can hear it. They can see it.

That's just the way it is with barrier breakers. Like Joshua and Caleb in ancient times, and like Chuck Yeager in more modern times, not many are willing to do things differently in order to conquer new frontiers. But Promised Land living is reserved for those with a "different spirit" (Num. 14:24, 30). The "one-in-a-millions" are the only ones who can expect to see different results, the kind that make others sit up and notice.

We've spent the better part of our time together talking about what it takes to grow personally intimate with God, to lose ourselves in His larger will for our lives, trusting Him through shadow and storm to give us everything we need in order to live in faith and abundance, no matter our circumstances. We've watched God deliver His people from Egypt, marveling again at how He's also delivered us from our sin and rebellion, drawing us into relationship with Himself through Christ Jesus and astounding us with grace too beautiful to resist. We've watched Him develop the children of Israel through their time spent in the wilderness, proving to us that His promises remain true even when everything seems to be going in the opposite direction.

Yes, deliverance is what makes this journey possible. And the development phase is what makes it profitable. But the bigger question now before us, as people who've been promised not just "life" but life "abundantly"—both the milk *and* the honey—is whether or not we'll be the one with a "different spirit." The uncommon, unique, and unusual ones who will go all the way with God. All the way to our appointed, abundant destiny.

Nearly all of us have experienced His leading us into the wilderness against our private wishes and personal preferences. With our pride and independent streak thus exposed, He has revealed Himself to us not only as our sole rock and resource but also as a God who is passionate about drawing us near, wanting us close. Will we follow Him now to the exclusion of all others, including the tyrant whose face is reflected in our bathroom mirror? Will we break the barriers that keep us from tasting and seeing, from knowing and experiencing Him? Will we be wholly dissatisfied with simply being part of a crowd—people who merely have a religious side to our lives, smiling and shaking hands and thinking the pew is probably enough for us?

Will we let deliverance and development lead us to the place where we are willing to get into the cockpit, alone if necessary, and burst into our destiny?

After many years of playing these issues somewhere in the middle, I can tell you now with total confidence in God's grace and power exactly where I stand on these questions. I am determined to be a woman who walks in the fruit of the Spirit He is growing within me. I want to be one who listens for His voice and expects to hear it, who believes what most others are only willing to wonder about. I want to be the one who is willing to anticipate His possibility in my impossibility. I want to be a magnet, not to draw people toward noticing Priscilla, but to draw down the presence of the Holy Spirit in such tangible ways that He cannot help but be seen in me. I want to be open to His gifts operating in my life and be willing to use them for the edification of His body. I want to be the one-in-a-million of whom others say, "There's something different about her. She's not just a Christian in name only. She's someone who experiences the power of God on a daily basis. He is her life. You can see it all over her."

I want it all. And all for His glory.

What about you? And what are you waiting for? Now is the time to make a move. It certainly was for ancient Israel, and it is for us as well. After eleven months of camping at the farthest point from Canaan, after hearing God's voice and seeing Him descend upon the mountain, after receiving the law and entering into covenant, the people had been deemed ready by God to restart their pilgrimage to the Promised Land. Having invited them to experience Him in the wilderness, He now had something more in store. He said to the children of Israel, "You have stayed long enough at this mountain" (Deut. 1:6). And when God has accomplished what He has set out to do in this season of life, He says the same to us. What we do at that moment will tell us whether or not we've decided that we've been through enough or that we've finally decided to break through the barriers—the ones that keep us stationed outside our destiny, perhaps for a lifetime.

The winds are changing.

New things are on the horizon.

Time to break camp.

> Turn and set your journey, and go to the hill country of the
> Amorites, and to all their neighbors in the Arabah, in the hill
> country and in the lowland and in the Negev and by the seacoast,
> the land of the Canaanites, and Lebanon, as far as the great river,
> the river Euphrates. (Deut 1:7)

"Turn . . . set . . . and go." All action verbs. All requiring a deliberate response from the people who were hearing them. Eleven months in the fearsome yet inviting presence of God at Sinai wasn't easy to turn their back on. No, it wasn't Egypt. And, no, it wasn't the Promised Land. But it had been their world for nearly a full year. It had become their new normal. Getting to Canaan, however, would require a willingness to accept a new normal, to break camp, turn from their usual activities, set a new plan, and go toward their destination. Reaching Canaan was reserved for those willing to make changes. God was calling them to another unknown and was preparing them to approach it by telling them to be thoughtful about their next steps. Moving toward Canaan would demand that they engage themselves mind, body, and spirit in a new undertaking. They must begin now to calculate their transition from development to destiny.

There comes a time in each of our walks with God when the season of camping out at the foot of Sinai ends, when we are compelled to take what we've gathered from drawing close to Him and start to move forward. Though wilderness circumstances are uniquely able to strip away our distractions and sharpen our focus on God's faithfulness, love, and glory—and though He uses these situations to help us learn to walk again in the relationship He desires—we must answer the stirring of His Spirit when He gently nudges us to the next place, a new place, in our journey.

Turn. Set. Go. Break camp, as well as the remaining barriers.

And so the question: Are you coming? Are you prepared to do things different? To turn away from your comfortable places, or perhaps from a certain sin or spiritual distraction, moving toward the place where God wants to take you? Are you willing to calculate how you intend to set yourself in a new direction, mapping out a plan of action that will help you make the transition? Are you not only willing to go where He is leading but also to be held accountable for following through?

God is calling. He's calling all those with a different spirit. The time has come. Turn, set, and go.

## The Mother of All Changes

As I've said before, motherhood has been something God has used to teach me dramatic spiritual lessons. When my first child arrived, I mistakenly thought I could continue as usual and still be the kind of mother he needed me to be. I quickly became aware, however, that this was impossible. The footloose, fancy-free schedule I was accustomed to following, as well as the loose-leaf method I had chosen for organizing and managing our home, became inadequate to meet these new challenges. That was pretty obvious now. My love for spontaneity fell victim to a nap and feeding schedule that left little room for change and variety. And my usual inattention to detail, which had basically become my default setting throughout life, now caused me to spend more time looking for stuff than looking after my baby. After six months, I'm sad to admit that much of my joy and excitement had been replaced by an overwhelming mix of fatigue and frustration.

How well I remember a particular afternoon when I came home from running errands, turned on my computer, and found an e-mail that proved to be God's word to me for that day. Like a swift kick in the backside, this message from a dear, older woman in the faith communicated something I dreaded yet desperately needed to hear. She suggested that the difficulties I was experiencing as a new mom really had little to do with parenting. The goal of achieving sane, successful motherhood was simply the laboratory where God was teaching me to be willing to turn from one way of living to another. I was being trained as a new mom how to respond to His direction so that I could be prepared to respond to any path His Spirit led me to walk, whenever and whatever that may be.

I just wanted to keep things like they were, to stay the same as I'd always been. But that wasn't going to work. Not now. What I had been doing worked for where I used to be, but going to this new place with Him—the place He had called me to follow—demanded that I make a deliberate decision to act in conjunction with the new goals He had set before me. And if I didn't choose to cooperate with what He was asking of me in the present, I would never work myself loose from the downward cycle of dissatisfaction I was enduring.

Motherhood is indeed a joyful experience but not for those who refuse to "turn, set, and go" within a new set of parameters. My personality is averse to change. I like things to stay the way they've always been. So in regard to making the transition to motherhood, it was hard for me to "turn" away from one way of living to another. As long as I rebelled against what this new season of life required, I was agitated and unable to relax in God's journey for me. But after finally making the decision to turn, the "setting" and "going" part of the equation—charting out a plan of action and following it—was at least doable.

Motherhood taught me a lesson that applied to my spiritual life as well. God's gifts require lifestyle modifications if we are to capably handle, enjoy, and appreciate fully what He is doing in our lives.

What situation are you in right now that's going to require a "turning" if you're ever able to embrace the will of God for your life? What kind of changes is He asking for? And what do you expect will happen if you continue resisting this new direction for whatever reason—inconvenience, fear of the unknown, distaste for the whole situation?

Paul speaks of how we are to "run in such a way" not merely to *survive* the race but to run with purpose and persistence—to run "that you may win" (1 Cor. 9:24). And the writer of Hebrews gives us specific instructions on how to do it (Heb. 12:1–2):

- Turn—"Let us also lay aside every encumbrance and the sin which so easily entangles us . . ."
- Set—"Fixing our eyes on Jesus, the author and perfecter of faith . . ."
- Go—"Let us run with endurance the race that is set before us."

God was moving Israel from one place to the next, preparing to put them into position where their hoped-for destiny would be clearly within reach. But in order to go where God was leading them, they were being told to take dynamic action, to do things differently than they had before. They were being expected to believe that what He had called them to conquer next was worth every challenge. They were being instructed to march boldly out of safety into a new phase of following Him. Breaking barriers depended on it.

## New Ways of Doing Things

Several years ago it seemed as though God was transitioning us into a new dimension of service in our ministry. One that would require us to change the methods and procedures that had been effective up till now but wouldn't be enough to accommodate the plans God was sharing with us for the near future. In so many areas,

He was asking us to trust Him more fully, rely on Him more completely, and anticipate His activity more readily.

He seemed eager to teach me a spiritual lesson at our first ministry event that year. He put me in front of a group of women I would normally not have been invited to address. I had accepted the invitation because I believed it was part of what God was doing in my life, but it was definitely out of my comfort zone. I don't mind admitting that I was much more nervous than usual about the entire thing.

And God wasn't helping matters much. Because right before speaking, I began feeling that tug of Holy Spirit conviction that stirs in just about every teacher's heart at some time or another—the persuasive inclination that I needed to change my message to something I hadn't prepared.

Big decision. Big risk. Big-time soul-searching.

The direction God seemed to be leading me was toward speaking about the woman caught in adultery in John 8 and about the grace Jesus extended toward her. I was familiar with the passage, of course. I knew the general principles I'd heard preached and taught on this New Testament text. But I had no outline ready for presenting a coherent talk on it. I reluctantly followed God's leading. And after giving the message, I felt pretty sure I had made a huge mess of the whole evening.

Nice try being spiritual.

The following week I received a letter from a woman who had been in attendance that night. She told me in her note that on the day prior to this particular event, the dirty little secret she had been fighting to keep quiet—the illicit affair she was actively engaged in—had been brought into the light. The threat of losing her husband of twenty years and their family of three children was now very real as a result of this revelation.

She hadn't planned on coming to this conference. But with her emotions a confusing blur of remorse and desperation, she had changed her mind and decided to attend. Maybe this would help her be able to sort some things out, if not at least keep her from having to be alone for the weekend. But when the Holy Spirit began reaching out to her through the message He had inspired me to give, she knew God was speaking directly into her heart. As I talked about the grace that Jesus extended to the woman in John 8, she felt His grace being poured out on her.

Chills raced down my spine as I read her letter. I could do nothing more than lay it down on the kitchen table, bury my head in my hands, and cry. I realized afresh that going forward with God is often an exercise in being led toward uncharted, uncomfortable territory. But when we follow the winds of His Spirit with a willingness to do whatever He says in this new season of servanthood, He takes us to places we've never been before and accomplishes tasks in and through us we could've never anticipated. To fail at following because of fear and resistance is to miss out on the glories of abundant life.

## Maintaining the Connection

Moments like these—times when God prepares us to go to the next leg in our journey—remind us why Sinai is so important. The intimacy God invites us to experience with Him in our darkest, driest, dustiest seasons is not some isolated occurrence. It's not as though we're supposed to walk ahead merely remembering what it was like to be there when God met us in our pain and brokenness and reestablished our relationship. Like the Hebrews emerging from Sinai, we're not simply to march onward but to march onward with *God*. We're not to leave His presence behind us at the mountain. We will find ourselves lost and gasping for breath before we know it if we think we can move ahead without maintaining our continued connection with Him. The fellowship and faith garnered at the Mountain of God are designed to keep us from rocking off balance when the new possibilities (as well as the new obstacles) of entering our destiny begin to appear.

Faced with this new direction to take, we are as much at risk of failure by steaming ahead in our own strength as we are by hanging back and letting the opportunity pass. When we sense God moving, when we suspect He is calling us toward a new phase of spiritual life, it's not just something to "get on with." If we let our intimacy with God diminish into mere details and to-do lists—if the focus becomes more on the "turning, setting, and going" than on the One who's calling us onto the path—we'll soon find ourselves alone and out ahead of God.

The pew is supposed to lead to a daily experience. Special times with God do not simply create fuel for us to burn until we can connect with Him again down the line, when we feel the need to stop by again for a fill-up. Intimacy with God is like carrying our energy source around with us at all times, continually replenished, never lacking for what we really need. It's sort of like my husband's Mophie, a battery that attaches to his iPhone and gives it hours and hours of extra life without having to be plugged in or recharged. Long after my phone has gone dead, Jerry's is still going strong, always charged and ready for use.

Bottom line: staying close to God—the way we were when He met us at our lowest point, at our Sinai—must remain a priority if we expect to keep experiencing Him. Abundant life is not borrowed from yesterday's surplus; it's rekindled by today's consistent supply.

And that means Promised Land living is right at your fingertips if you want it and if you're willing to receive it on God's terms. The invitation to break camp and head toward abundant living is not just for the paid staff. Not just for the seminary trained. Not just for those who seem like they always know what to do when it comes to spiritual matters. God's calling, provision, and plan are for everyone who claims Christ Jesus as Savior and Lord.

The words Moses spoke at the beginning of Deuteronomy 1 were to "all Israel" (v. 1). It's an expression used more than a dozen times throughout this book of the Bible. The appeal was for every person in the nation. It didn't single out the Levitical priests or just a few of God's favorite tribes. Every person from every division of the nation—from the youngest to the oldest—was invited to reach his or her destiny. Truly God's invitation to experience the milk and honey of Canaan is not for a select few but for all who have been delivered from Egypt's hold of slavery. Whatever your past or even your present shortcomings, the opportunity to go forth with God, walking in the new way of His Spirit, is extended to you and to anyone willing to turn, set, and go His way.

I can't begin to tell you how many times I've felt as though God's promises were not for me. I often assumed that the people I saw who were walking with Him in obvious ways—those who were experiencing His presence and power, seeing His activity and hearing His voice, walking by His Spirit and exercising His fruit and gifts with bold confidence and consistency—hadn't done some of things I'd done. They had made better use of God's grace in their lives, I reasoned—unlike me, who had wasted a lot of what He had invested on stubborn rebellion and resistance.

But think of what you know about Israel, just over the course of time since they'd left Egypt. Yahweh's anger had been aroused more than once because of their poor choices and their stiff-necked response to His activity in their lives. Yet here they were, leaving Sinai as one people, chosen and unified by God's sovereign love, each of them equal recipients of the covenant He had made with them at the mountain. Yes, their obedience would be required if they expected to enjoy Promised Land living to its fullest extent. But the invitation to come and walk in it was laid on the table for all.

His grace eliminates the ultimate barrier.

Yet in order for us to embrace this opportunity and make it our own, He calls us to participate with Him in this abundant life experience through a deliberate decision to "turn, set, and go." He has done all that is necessary for us to trust Him. He has proven His faithfulness, His steadfastness, His supernatural desire to seek intimacy with mortal men and women. Nothing is left but what He knows is best for us—our total buy-in to the blessings He has promised by hitching our hearts to His wagon and marching on to His grace-filled destiny.

So why stay back behind the barricades? Why forsake the milk and honey, settling for a menu that's much more tasteless and much less satisfying? You have been here "long enough." Don't run back inside when God has told you to break camp. Step out onto the road to Canaan. Welcome the winds of change.

*Do you not know that in a race all the runners compete, but only one receives the prize? So run that you may obtain it.*

1 CORINTHIANS 9:24 ESV

## CHAPTER 13

# Oasis of Complacency

YOU'RE NOT GOING TO BELIEVE THIS.

The Hebrews made it to the edge of Canaan somewhere between fifteen and eighteen months after leaving Egypt.

Yup, you heard me right. The Scriptures tell us it was "eleven days' journey from Horeb [Sinai] by the way of Mount Seir to Kadesh-barnea" (Deut. 1:2). Eleven days. That means it took less than two weeks after breaking camp at Sinai, where they'd spent about a year, for the Hebrews to reach this entry point on the southern border of Canaan.

Get this time stamp in your mind because it's one of the more overlooked, miscalculated bits of information about this whole era in Israel's history. In relative terms it hadn't been that long from the events of the actual exodus to this moment when God positioned His people at the brink of the Promised Land, at Kadesh-barnea. No more than a year and a half.

But if you think *that* little piece of biblical trivia is surprising, get ready for the most bewildering of all. It was here—orbiting in a fairly tight circle around Kadesh-barnea and the larger general area, the wilderness of Paran—where the children of Israel would wander for the *next thirty-eight years!*

Contrary to what most of us tend to think, their wilderness meanderings didn't take them all over the map. They were *right there* the whole time—a skip and a jump from steaming full sail into the land of milk and honey, armed with the ironclad security of His trustworthy promises. Instead they proved in living color the spiritual truth we've noticed before: the barrier to Promised Land living is not the wilderness; the barrier is *wandering* in the wilderness.

And it took them nearly forty years to figure that out.

Why would anyone settle for circles when milk and honey were within arms' reach?

It could be that Kadesh-barnea wasn't a bad place to be. Turns out, the edge of the Promised Land is a pretty nice place to hang out. Kadesh-barnea was an oasis, and nearby areas east of the Jordan were plush and comfortable. It benefited from the nutrient-rich soil and healthy landscaping that was inherent from its nearness to Canaan's agricultural plenty. Located just outside a land of unparalleled fullness, this spot possessed enough clear water and comfortable living conditions to make it an easy place in which to settle down and stay. Circling around an oasis seemed preferable to taking a straight line to potential abundance.

I don't know how to describe how much this distresses me— mostly because it has often described me. Too many believers continue to model the actions exhibited by the Hebrews. God has granted them a bit of victorious living and oasis refreshment, and they get settled and content on the outer fringes of abundant life, feeling as though they've got all of God they really want or need. They're pretty much OK with the way things are, not really believing or even desiring more than what just comes from showing up dressed every morning. In fact, if they were being perfectly honest, they think that people who do venture out boldly with God are taking this faith thing a little too far, to the point of being foolish. They'd be a bit embarrassed, frankly, to carry on like that.

So give them Kadesh-barnea—a good conference, a Christian book, spiritual music, an up year at church, an up year of victorious Christian living, or just a good day—and that seems to do the trick. Before you know it, they're settled in for the long haul. The desire for more is gone in a flash. Oasis accommodations suit them just fine. May as well look into the long-term rates—by the month, by the year. There are all sorts of packages like these to choose from at the oasis of complacency.

Be honest. Is that where you are right now on your journey with God? Perhaps? Not sure? Truth is, we've all been there, and it's really not that hard to tell when we are. Here are some things that might indicate you've gotten comfortable just east of the Jordan.

*You might be in the oasis of complacency* if the Promised Land is starting to look way too risky, if you've decided it's really not worth what it costs to go to the next level with God. I'm sure you remember earlier in the book when we talked about needing to leave behind the places where the enemy reigns. Well, he reigns in the oasis of complacency. He hates to see any Christian entering new territory with God. He'll try everything he can think of to diminish your desire for pressing on and following through. And few of his schemes work more effectively than the disguise of complacency. He makes the adventure of discovering new levels in God look too risky, far too costly and makes your current, boring, unimaginative surroundings look strangely spectacular. This is where he wants you. Stuck here. And when left to our own flesh and desires, we're comfortable letting him lure us into it.

In fact, two and a half tribes of Israel knew exactly what this is like. The trans-Jordanic area near the oasis at Kadesh was famous for its rich and extensive pastures. It would lure Reuben, Gad, and half of the tribe of Manasseh. These tribes were incredibly blessed with large herds and flocks so the plush vegetation and rich pasture of the land east of Canaan was especially inviting. Moses suspected that they made this special request to be able to stay on this side of the Jordan River in an attempt to escape the risky warfare that was sure to arrive once they stepped foot on the west side (Num. 32). On the edge of abundance, they elected to stay permanently on the east side of the Jordan River instead of pressing into the depths of the Promised Land. They had become satisfied with safety. Comfortable with the common. They chose not to go into the Promised Land, charmed by the satisfying allure of this area.

Have you settled for less than the fullness of what God is offering? Have you become complacent with *good* while *best* is just around the next bend? Are you unwilling to walk away from some things you've grown accustomed to, things that are apparently more valuable to you than the experience of being intimately related with God on a daily, hourly basis? If so, you've wandered into Kadesh-barnea. And you're not likely to want to leave.

*You might be in the oasis of complacency* if you've started thinking you've arrived and that nothing more is really required of you at this point in life. You've basically stopped hungering for anything new, concluding that your present experience with God is probably as good as it's going to get.

A complete conquest of the Promised Land didn't happen the second the Israelites stepped on Canaan's soil. The territory actually conquered and possessed in the time of Joshua was much less than what was promised to Israel. Even in the time of David and Solomon, when the land reached its greatest extent, they never completely controlled the outlying districts. Will the nation of Israel ever fully possess the land? The prophets have declared that at the time of Christ's return to Earth, He will regather the Jews and will reign in the land over a converted and redeemed Israel. Full and complete possession of the land awaits that day (see Jer. 16:14–16; Amos 9:11–15; Zech. 8:4–8).[17] So in the biblical record there was always more ground to cover, always more territory to traverse. They never "arrived." They had to keep pressing on.

What does this mean for us? Our journey toward completely conquering the abundant life will never be a done deal on this side of heaven. As believers who want to claim what is rightfully ours, we must make a decision to take steps of faith by the Spirit's power every day for the rest of our lives. There is always new territory in God to cover. This journey is a lifelong commitment.

So if you've decided you don't need to go any farther—whether from pride in your own accomplishments or simply from the loss of spiritual appetite—then you've spread your blanket short of the Promised Land. And there's a good chance you'll be content to picnic here for a long, long time. Perhaps your whole lifetime.

*You might be in the oasis of complacency* if the enemy rarely hinders your progress in any noticeable way. As long as the children of Israel were on the opposite side of the Jordan River, they weren't bothered by the inhabitants of Jericho or Ai. But when they finally did venture into Canaan, it wasn't long at all before they'd met up with their first big enemy challenge. When the battle against temptation is no longer much of a battle anymore, when you don't spend time engaging in the spiritual warfare that used to feel like a constant need in your life, if the devil is not working your nerves day in and day out, you'll know you're probably not in the midst of Promised Land living. In Canaan it's like the enemy is always on your trail. You're having to fight him all day long with the Word of God, keeping your mind squared away on the Spirit, taking every thought captive and making it obey Christ. You can feel Satan warring against your family, your finances, and everything that's going on around you.

No one ever said the approach to Canaan or living in Canaan would be a walk in the park. It requires standing guard against enemies on the ground as well as enemies in the heart. Each day when the children of Israel set out from the night's rest, Moses would offer these watchwords as both a prayer and a reminder of what they could expect on the other side: "Rise up, O LORD! And let Your enemies be scattered, and let those who hate You flee before You" (Num. 10:35). This was military language. Battle readiness. He was very aware—and trying to help the people see—that any progress toward the Promised Land would be met with powerful attempts at thwarting their advance.

But not by the pools of Kadesh-barnea. Life in the oasis of complacency is usually marked by limited enemy opposition—which might be nice if it weren't also limited in terms of exhilaration, joy, purpose, and the experience of God's supernatural power.

Don't settle, my friend. Be one-in-a-million.

Want it. Risk it. It is so, so worth it.

## Promised Land Living

The radical believers whose relationships with God have most impacted me are those who are not satisfied with any oasis outside of Canaan no matter how refreshing and temporarily satisfying it may be. They are willing to be the one-in-a-million, to believe Him in ways that most would never dare to do. I think of a certain new friend of mine who has faced one hardship after another on her fearless journey to and through Canaan. Financial challenges. Health problems. A child in drug rehab. And yet the extent of her faith in a limitless God refuses to let her sink into either complacency or despair. I've stood by in prayer with her, watching on more than one occasion when their family's home was a day away from foreclosure. But time and again through the miracle working of God, enough money arrived, a delay was called, paperwork fell through. She's experiencing Promised Land living, with all its obstacles and challenges, and wouldn't trade it for even a weekend stay outside the borders of God's blessing, out in Kadesh-barnea.

I think of another close friend whose life seems to be filled with heartache after heartache. After years of praying that God would enable her to lay aside her full-time, bill-paying job in order to come home and spend more time mothering her daughter, things all finally came together. What a relief and blessing it was to be released from this season in her life, no longer separated from what she felt called to do. But almost immediately after changing her daily routine from workplace to full-time homemaking, she was diagnosed with rheumatoid arthritis. The physical pain and exhaustion severely challenged her ability to take full advantage of what she had long hoped to do. On the heels of this news, she faced another huge setback when her husband admitted to being involved sexually with another woman. He was leaving home and turning his back on their marriage and family.

I'd be lying to say that she doesn't wonder—as all of us do—why God has seen fit to allow grave problems like these to beset such a lovely, faith-filled woman. She grows tired of girding for the battle each day. But I can tell you she's in the minority of people who stare into the teeth of pain and loss and exclaim that she will not be overwhelmed by the enemy's size and numbers. Her sense of peace, joy, and strength reveal that in spite of difficulty, she's an inhabitant of the Promised Land. Despite her trying circumstances, she still has complete trust in her Master, a total confidence that He will care for her and lead her safely on to the destination He desires for her. The faith built within her at the Red Seas and Marahs of her life, as well as the intimacy God has established with her at Sinai, have kept her relationship with Him top priority, no matter how early it means getting up in the morning or how much more logical it might seem to try another way. Even with circumstances worsening, I've heard her say to me, "I still expect and fully anticipate that God can do a miracle. I believe that all of this has got to be for something bigger than I can even imagine."

Promised Land living. This is what it looks like. Not easy chairs. Not happy-go-lucky. No, it's something far superior to that. Promised Land living is power, confidence, endurance, thankfulness. It's spiritual fruit growing right at your fingertips. It's boldness that can't be shaken by anything, even when an earthquake is erupting all around you. No matter the noise level and magnitude. It's forgiveness, freedom, full expectation. It's strapping on the armor and daring any devil in hell to try defeating what God is accomplishing in you. Promised Land living is both loud and quiet, tough and tender; it's everything you need it to be. It's here. It's now. And how! And *wow!* No comparison. No complaints. Please—no more complacency.

Oh, how I long to be like these dear sisters—and others, though few and far between—who are willing to go against the grain of the culture, even against the grain of other Christians sometimes. While most choose to handle their spiritual disciplines with dutiful indifference, these women race into the arms of God with desperate abandon. While most play it safe in the comfort zones of Christianity, these women choose to take risks and stand alone if necessary to do it.

They're in the minority. And they're fine with that. If the alternative is Kadesh-barnea, everybody else can just have it.

## Cluster Keepers

So how'd all this wandering business around the oasis of complacency begin?

So glad you asked.

Kadesh-barnea was situated at the northernmost point of the Wilderness of Paran, the place where we catch up with Moses and the children of Israel at the beginning of Numbers 13. When they first arrived, little more than a year into the journey, God instructed Moses to call out spies to cross over and get a firsthand glimpse of Canaan, the land "which I am going to give to the sons of Israel" (v. 2). Sounds like pretty much a done deal to me. That was the mission—to go and get an initial taste of the plenty they had been both promised and provided.

But beginning in verse 17, Moses' instructions to the spies implied that if the land looked impregnable, he would be hesitant to launch an immediate assault. He and the people saw this fact-finding mission as a means of determining whether or not to enter the land at all instead of a simple means of planning the best way to go about doing what God had told them. So it was little wonder, when the party returned giving their mixed report, that they took it as reason enough to back off, to stand down, to give these radical promises of God a little time to be thought through and analyzed.

> They told him, and said, "We went in to the land where you sent us; and it certainly does flow with milk and honey, and this is its fruit. Nevertheless, the people who live in the land are strong, and the cities are fortified and very large; and moreover, we saw the descendants of Anak there. Amalek is living in the land of the Negev and the Hittites and the Jebusites and the Amorites are living in the hill country, and the Canaanites are living by the sea and by the side of the Jordan." (Num. 13:27–29)

Yikes. Didn't expect that.

Yes, they had found some amazing specimens of the plenty Canaan could produce, particularly at the Valley of Eschol—a word that means "cluster"—where a single cutting of grapes taken from the vines there was so plump and luscious it had to be carried on a pole between two men. That's a lot of fruit, not to mention the pomegranates and figs and other things they found growing in profusion.

These men, each of them leaders from among their respective tribes (see v. 2), held in their hands the visible proof of both the goodness and the reliability of God. What He had told them in Egypt had proven 100 percent true: the land certainly did "flow with milk and honey." They admitted as much. And yet . . .

"Nevertheless."

If there's a single word that doomed this generation of God's people from experiencing Promised Land living in their lifetime, it's this one: "nevertheless." They had heard with their own ears the assurances of God. They had seen and certainly tasted the cluster of fruit that more than verified, beyond their wildest imaginations, just how accurate God had been when He had described the land to them. They had sat on the proverbial pew at Sinai, basking in His glory, hearing His voice, seeing His power descend from on high, just as He does when we sit in our churches Sunday after Sunday. And yet . . .

Nevertheless.

This was the word that turned a forty-day excursion into a forty-year, self-imposed death sentence. The people saw, but they chose not to believe. Let's just call it what it is. They chose the oasis of complacency. They chose less than God's best. They chose to concede defeat.

They chose wrong.

And "nevertheless," we're still capable of keeping up the error of their ways. We can so easily be complacent in the same, scaredy-cat approach to life. It's not hard to become a "nevertheless" Christian.

Maybe you're facing some things in your marriage right now that are truly horrible and frightening. You've heard that God can do amazing things with situations like these, but—nevertheless—yours just seems beyond His repair.

Maybe you have a wayward child who's decided to live a life-style that's totally different from the way you raised and taught your family. You've heard that God can bring the prodigal home, but—nevertheless—you don't expect it to happen for you and your child. If people could hear the way your son talks, if they knew the things your daughter was doing, they'd feel the same way. There's *no* way.

Maybe the doctors have confirmed a bad prognosis on your health or that of someone you love. You've heard that God is a healer, One who can still perform wonders in the face of grim reports and cloudy X-ray readings, but—nevertheless—you're not inclined even to ask Him about that. You don't think this applies to your situation.

The simplest place in the world to live is in the oasis of complacency, whose capital city must certainly be named "Nevertheless." God may do things for other people. He may work through the person on that end of the pew, the one with all the talent and personality and friends and faith. But He's not liable to work through you. Besides, those clusters of fruit they possess aren't worth hazarding all the Hittites and Jebusites and Amorites and such like.

I've thought those things. I've said those things.

Maybe what you and I need right now to change this way of thinking—to kick-start our plans for going to the Promised Land—is to pull out that cluster of proof that speaks volumes to the goodness of God. Firsthand things. Forgotten things. Even if your recent days have been filled with frustrations and disappointments, I still know you can look back and find evidence of God's promises to you. Not one or two. Not a tiny handful, measured in ounces, carried easily in a grocery sack. What God gives, He gives in clusters. And if we're smart, we'll keep a list of these in our Bibles or personal journals where we can always go to be reminded of how many ways He has proven His faithfulness and provision.

May we never, like the distrusting spies sent to scope out the Promised Land, hold these huge bunches of God's blessing in our hands and not believe that He can conquer whatever enemies we'll be called upon to face.

## Little Help?

I don't know what God has been doing in your heart throughout this book, particularly in this one chapter where I've intended to pull back the blinders on a shortchanged lifestyle decision that is so easy and natural to make and so hard to pull out of. There's not one of us who hasn't caved to complacency. We've all had our mail addressed to us in Kadesh-barnea before.

But I just want to encourage you. You don't have to stay there. Moving out is no easy matter, that's for sure. But we're all in this together, my friend. And there are people in your life who would love to come alongside and help you if you'd admit what needs repairing, if you'd be honest about what you're lacking and serious about setting a new course for Canaan.

We recently moved to a fairly rural section of the Dallas/Fort Worth area, which has been just great for the boys to have space to run around in and for Jerry and me to enjoy the peace and quiet. But one of the things that's been a little hard getting used to, after years of living closer to the city, is not having high-speed Internet access. We had it at our old house, but in our first weeks of moving into the new one, Jerry spent hours on the phone with different companies trying to figure out how to get us going on the information highway. It was frustrating. Even my wireless card was sort of a hit-and-miss operation, depending on which way the wind was blowing, I guess.

Thank God, then, for Rachel. She lives directly across from us in a house that's somehow positioned in such a way that the high-speed works perfectly. I can't count the times I've asked her if I can come over and mooch off her Internet availability. She lets me bring my laptop and baby Jude over and sit right there at her kitchen table to work and read e-mails. In fact, I think she just expects me now because she's put a little lamp near the place where I usually sit. She's made a spot for me in her life. It's so nice just to walk across the street and get a little bit of what she has to offer.

You may be at a place in life where you're needing some high-speed peace and joy, not to mention a few other spiritual assets that are missing from your current account balance. You once had them yourself, but some things have gotten moved around in your life lately, and you just can't seem to pick them up like you used to. What you may need is someone nearby who wouldn't mind at all if you called them up and asked if you could just mooch a little from their supply of faith and biblical perspective.

I hope you'll take me up on this. Because the oasis of complacency is no place to stay. And sometimes we need a little help getting out of it.

It's worth any risk and time expense to put Kadesh-barnea behind you and out of your bloodstream. The fruits of God's promises are waiting for you in Canaan, as well as—yes—probably the fight of your life. But it's better than dying a slow death at a place that was never meant to be more than a rest stop. Complacency would love to see you stay. Your Lord is calling you away.

Come out of Kadesh-barnea and live.

*"Forget about what's happened; don't keep going over old history. Be alert, be present. I'm about to do something brand-new. It's bursting out! Don't you see it? There it is! I'm making a road through the desert, rivers in the badlands."*

ISAIAH **43:18–19** *THE MESSAGE*

CHAPTER 14

# Out with the Old

I HOPE YOU'VE FELT A little staleness in the oasis air after reading the last chapter—a scent of sameness you hadn't really noticed before but one that now seems terribly distasteful with the aromas of the Promised Land so surprisingly close.

I hope when the curtains were thrown back on your accommodations east of the Jordan, the fresh rays of light revealed rooms in dire need of updating, with walls just begging to be painted in the bright new colors of Canaan.

I hope that being only a few steps away from abundant living has caused your heart to churn within you as the Spirit allures you to press ahead, to enter into a life overflowing with power and spiritual plenty.

The humdrum oasis just doesn't cut it anymore, does it?

I hope it doesn't.

Oh, how I pray it never does again.

If there's only going to be one-in-a-million, don't you want it to be you?

Then you can't do what you've always done and hope it takes you in a new direction. Einstein called this the definition of insanity: "doing the same thing over and over again and expecting different results." In fact, the only way to truly live is to pass through a valley of death, of sorts. To the early Israelites, this meant coming face-to-face with the most shocking death of all.

The last few verses of Deuteronomy stunned the nation of Israel with the following news: Moses was dead (Deut. 34:5). He had been their established leader every day since they had left Egypt in triumph forty years before.

A lot of experiences were tied up in their relationship together as God's ambassador and God's people—some of them remarkable, some of them regrettable. Yet he had always been their hope for the future. They were assured that keeping their step in line with Moses would surely, someday, lead them into the abundance Yahweh had promised them long ago. But now Moses was gone. And when he died, so did a big chunk of the people's hope. In fact, his loss caused such great anguish from one end of the Hebrew camp to the other that the Scripture says, "The sons of Israel wept for Moses in the plains of Moab thirty days" (Deut. 34:8).

This might seem like an insignificant bit of information, but it isn't. Tradition in Old Testament times called for the official period of mourning to last only about *seven* days. But Moses' death was no ordinary event. Mourning him was no ordinary event either. He had not just been a man who gave them directions for the journey; he was their hope of Canaan. How many times had he been the mediator between them and the wrath of God? How many times had their journey been made easier because God used Moses as a miracle-working tool? They'd felt safe following him all these years. Having experienced success and survival in their journey this far, the people certainly thought that continued victory could only be achieved as they followed him. That's why when he died, seven days stretched to thirty—why a week stretched to a month. And I don't think anyone could fault them for that.

Major losses take time to get over, especially when the thing you've lost is what has kept you going thus far and what you expected to keep you going until the end. It's somewhat shocking to realize that the things you've been depending on to keep your spiritual life on course have been good enough up till now, but something new is going to be required if you want to keep moving forward.

The death of Israel's hope wasn't easy for ancient Israel. The death of *your* "Moses" won't be easy either. But it's a requirement for anyone wanting to step foot on Canaan's soil.

## From Death to Life

You've already conceded that leaving Egypt to go on this journey with God has meant cutting off some bad things—hazardous sins, perhaps some unhealthy relationships, any number of hindrances that were keeping you from going where God was leading. But what about when the Lord shows you that even some *good* things, some Moses things, must die in order for you to step foot on Canaan's soil?

Maybe it's the comforts, traditions, and safety nets of your church-as-usual religion. Maybe it's one or more daily habits or mind-sets you've developed along the way. Maybe it's a box-check mentality you've been bringing to your devotional life, a method that has kept you in the Word but no longer *growing* in the Word. Not *bad* things. Just temporary things, yesterday's things. Things that were helpful, perhaps even needful for a part of the journey, but are not able to take you the rest of the way.

Maybe God is showing you that you've been placing too much confidence in another person to assist you in your journey. You thought, for example, that you'd finally found a church where they knew how to worship God the way you always dreamed it should happen. The pastor taught the Word there with a passion that made you never want to miss a Sunday. You'd even been known to tweak your vacation plans so you weren't away from home on the weekend. You didn't want to miss what he had to say. It felt like heaven on earth. You were growing by leaps and bounds. But then the pastor admitted some kind of moral failing that shook your faith in him and then in God. You discovered he wasn't the man you'd made him out to be. You thought this person would help lead you on to abundant living. You'd put your confidence in a person rather than God. Now this beloved pastor is out of your weekly routine, and the unexpected hole in your life has devastated you.

Losses like these hurt you. They aren't put behind you one afternoon and forgotten by morning. You are allowed time to grieve, just as Israel did. They probably entertained the notion that the Promised Land had been lost to them forever, now that Moses was gone. They had set their hopes on this man. How could they go on without him? Unthinkable. They had little to no perception of a future that didn't include him in it. Take their long-time leader out of the equation, and everything suddenly tumbles way off balance.

But God will do that sometimes when He knows we need it. He'll upset the standard way we've been practicing our life and Christian faith, the things we've been subtly and secretly putting our trust in, the things that feel comfortable to us but don't get us any closer to living in Canaan.

This doesn't usually call for a complete overhaul of our lives. It's not as though everything we've thought, done, or believed was wrong, as though all of life up till now has been lived in total error. But because we are "prone to wander," as the old hymn says—because we tend toward idolatry rather than a pure, undiluted, passionate pursuit of God—He will lead us to make adjustments to our expectations of what living with Him is all about. He'll do things to help us remember that we are "servants of a new covenant, not of the letter but of the Spirit; for the letter kills, but the Spirit gives life" (2 Cor. 3:6). He will allow the death of something, even if it's as seemingly innocent as our morning routine or our driving patterns or the way we spend our lunch hour, in order for us to take bold new steps in abundant living.

Moses must give way to Joshua.

I want you to see these two men of God, not just as two individuals but as representatives of two different types of expectations and ways of living—two lifestyles that describe how a person approaches and navigates their path. And the Moses lifestyle, though effective in many ways and appropriate for certain times of life, requires adjustment if a person hopes to escape the oasis and embrace the true milk and honey. The Moses lifestyle can take you part of the way, but some of it must be left behind if you expect to move ahead. To taste abundance on a daily basis, you and I need more of a Joshua lifestyle—a way of living we'll examine closely in the final chapter.

## Enough Is Enough

I'm telling you, the loss of some of these long-held habits and comfort points—some of these "deaths" that need to occur—will hurt for a while. Their absence may even be felt longer than you expect. Nothing wrong with that. In the case of Israel, the death of Moses caused them to grieve for an extended period of time. Seven days just wasn't quite adequate. But there came a time when enough was enough.

"The days of weeping and mourning for Moses came to an end" (Deut. 34:8).

At a certain point you must make a deliberate choice to move on, when you need to get beyond what you miss about the oasis and your time spent on the east side of the Jordan. There comes a time when the best advice anyone can give you is to just get over it. While each of us needs time to heal, we can't allow healthy mourning to become unhealthy sulking.

You see, mourning in ancient Israel wasn't merely a time of weeping. It included a number of cultural rituals that helped ancient people lament and grieve someone's passing. They would do things like tearing their clothes, dressing in sackcloth, sitting in sprinkled ashes, shaving their heads, sitting in silence for long periods of time. Wealthier Israelites, in fact, would even hire professional mourners to assist them in the task at hand.

So when the time for weeping came to an end, it meant they chose to stop participating in the *act* of mourning. And at some point, like the children of Israel, we too must choose not to participate in mournful acts anymore. This doesn't mean our hearts are no longer saddened or that tears no longer fall from our eyes. It just means we've stopped acting in a way that keeps us focused on what we've lost or left behind.

This isn't easy for me to suggest to you because it isn't easy for me to do. To stop *acting* sad when I *feel* sad is difficult. I still enjoy talking about the details of my hurt feelings on the phone with my girlfriends and rehearsing the issues in my mind, dwelling on the sacrifices I've made (or have been forced to make). But at some point mourning is no longer appropriate. We must move on. A new day is dawning. It always does when God is drawing us toward the Promised Land.

For directly on the heels of their sobering mood at the end of Deuteronomy 34:8—like a deep breath, a tissue, a splash of cool water on their faces—these words mark the beginning of verse 9:

"Now Joshua . . ."

Had their eyes still been full of verse 8's tears, their blurred vision might not have been able to see the gift described in verse 9. As close and comfortable as they had been with Moses, God was giving these people a new leader. Not just a new leader but a bold new paradigm to follow. Since God had not allowed Moses to enter Canaan, it was clear that following him and what he represented had only been able to take them so far—and no farther. To walk into the land of milk and honey, the people would need to set their hopes and attention on another leader who could take them the rest of the way. Yes, Moses had led them out of Egypt, had been bravely willing to implement an unpopular plan that took them in the opposite direction of Canaan, had faithfully delivered God's message to them at Sinai, and had moved them into position to take the Promised Land.

But that was it. Moses' style of leadership, while strong and valuable, had ultimately prevented the people from crossing over into abundance. Joshua's, on the other hand, invited it.

So God was leading His people to play the role of a trapeze artist, releasing their grip on the bar they'd been holding, swinging freely into midair high above the wilderness floor. An act like this would be undoable—unthinkable—unless they knew that someone they trusted was sending them another bar to grab onto. *He was.* God was providing them just the amount of thrust they needed to move from being wilderness wanderers to Canaan conquerors.

Yes, you can mourn and move on with your head up, my friend, because whatever you've had to release has only served to empty your hands for what He is about to give you. Your confidence can rest easy in Someone you trust. You can let go and fully believe that He is sending exactly what you need to carry you the rest of the way. The loss of Moses may be heartbreakingly difficult, but a new opportunity is on the horizon.

So what is He asking you to release?

Take courage, Promised Land pilgrim, and let go.

Joshua is coming.

*Now therefore arise, go over this Jordan, you and all this people,*
*into the land that I am giving to them, to the people of Israel.*
*Every place that the sole of your foot will tread upon I have*
*given to you, just as I promised to Moses.*

JOSHUA 1:2–3 ESV

CHAPTER 15

# A New and Living Way

NEAR OUR HOME IS A fishing pond, something like twenty-five
feet deep, where rumor has it that an infamously large bass lurks
untouched in its depths. People have seen him near the surface on
occasion, so they know he's down there. Fishermen have sat for long
periods of time, dangling all kinds of hooks and lures to try reeling
him in. Thus far, however, this fish has been able to avoid being
caught.

I took my boys over there recently. We sort of had hopes that we
might reel in the phantom monster from the deep. And we did have
a good day. Between them they hauled in a dozen nice catches—
a few small perch and sunfish—which was more than enough to
keep them laughing and happy. Yet I confess, I found myself looking
out over the still waters at times, peering down into the darkness,

wondering if the legendary, elusive bass would ever be seen on someone's hook.

There are lots of other fish in that pond. But only one like *him*.

Looking out over the millions of Hebrews perched at the mouth of the Promised Land, swimming in the grace and protection of Yahweh, you'd have been hard pressed to find one whose faith was worth catching. A quick look within the depths of the tent-lined camps would have left you extremely disappointed. Finding the elusive members of this nation who had a different spirit, who truly believed God, and who expected to live someday in the inheritance they'd been promised would have been a real long shot.

Still, there was one. (Two, actually—Joshua and Caleb.) Two out of the approximately two million adults who'd left Egypt, one of whom was given the task of leading God's people into their promised abundance.

One-in-a-million.

But what was it about Joshua that made him the standard of how Promised Land living is supposed to be sought for and acquired? What qualities of life did he possess that not only inspired the Hebrews finally to step over into Canaan but can also apply to our own selves as we desire to set our sights on the milk and honey? Let's follow along as the Bible presents him to us chronologically, revealing a progression of characteristics that must mark our lives if we plan to live the Promised Land life. Receive them as bold, active commands from your Father who longs for you to live in His milk-and-honey abundance.

## 1. Advance with Courage

The first time we lay eyes on Joshua is in Exodus 17. Most scholars believe that Joshua was approximately forty years old at the time of this event in his life. Like all the other refugees of his age in the

Hebrew camp, he had most likely spent his youth in the pits of Egypt making bricks. He was no military commander trained in the art of war and yet, camped at Rephidim, Moses told him to "choose men for us and go out, fight against Amalek." And, get this, "Joshua did as Moses told him." Just like that. No questions asked. He did it so courageously, in fact, that he "overwhelmed Amalek and his people with the edge of the sword" (vv. 9–10, 13). It's our first encounter with Joshua, and already it is immediately obvious that he is a brave, bold, valiant soul. Moses may have been the mouthpiece through which this commission came, but Joshua received it as coming from Yahweh Himself. And when told what to do, he did it. Fearlessly.

Joshua was the same age Moses was when, as a simple shepherd, he had heard God's voice coming from a burning bush, calling him to lead the Hebrews out of slavery in Egypt. Remember how Moses responded to this commission?

"What shall I say to them?" (Exod. 3:13).

"What if they will not believe me or listen to what I say?" (4:1).

"Please, Lord, I have never been eloquent, neither recently nor in time past, nor since You have spoken to Your servant; for I am slow of speech and slow of tongue" (4:10).

Not exactly the kind of heroic heartbeat we were hoping for.

Two men. Both called to lead God's people. Both required to wage war. Both made capable by God to handle the tasks of their assignment. But the similarities between the two stops there because without excuse and without delay, "Joshua did as Moses told him."

His quick acceptance shows more than just a willingness to obey. It shows unwavering courage in the face of risky circumstances. This is perhaps the primary characteristic that distinguished Moses and Joshua. One was unsure of himself and of God's ability while the other never questioned either. One was more concerned about who and what was against him while the other had confidence in the One who was *for* him. One sought to escape the duty of his calling because he felt incapable of fulfilling it, while the other faced it head-on despite his limited capability, trusting that God would take up the slack. Our first introduction to Joshua reveals a man who courageously engaged in the tasks he was divinely called to encounter. Moses, for all the mighty things God chose to do through him, was not always quick to operate this way.

Is there something in your life right now that God has called you to do, but you just don't have the courage to engage in? What do your excuses reveal about yourself and how you feel about God? For each of Moses' excuses, God had a response. It took time, but He assured Moses that human inability could never override God's divine ability to work through him and to accomplish His purposes. How much different, though, to be a person like Joshua who doesn't need coddling and explanations? Look what God can do through someone who receives His instructions not just personally . . . but fearlessly.

Fear does not come from God, the Scripture plainly tells us (2 Tim. 1:7). In fact, one of the ways I determine His will for my life is like this: if discerning His will means making a decision between two options, and my only reason for being suspicious of one of the options is that I'm afraid of it, I know this is probably the choice He's wanting me to make. If fear is the *only* reason I'm resistant to follow, I can usually assume the enemy is trying to keep me from doing what the Lord wants me to do. I'm learning that fear is a spirit given by the enemy to divert us away from God's will. He will often pervert the most sensitive area, the tender place of your life, by attaching fear to it because your area of sensitivity and tenderness is probably the area where God wants you to experience the most victory and through which He wants to produce the most effective ministry. This is why the enemy wants to stop you by making you afraid.

Think about the decisions you're needing to make. Is fear a major factor in causing you to shy away from one response or the other? Consider that maybe this is the enemy's attempt at keeping you from crossing the Jordan and walking fully into God's promises for you. Very often God doesn't call us to do the possible; He calls us (and equips us) to handle the impossible.

Fear not. Abandon any path, even if it's the easier path, that doesn't lead to abundance.

## 2. Accept Your Post

Look carefully at the assignments that were handed out in Exodus 17: "Joshua did as Moses told him and fought against Amalek; and Moses, Aaron and Hur went up to the top of the hill" (v. 10). Apparently, the job assignments were not the same for everyone.

Imagine Moses sitting in his tent, flanked by Aaron and Hur, telling Joshua to choose the fighting men and take them into battle at the risk of his own life—hardly the plum assignment compared with what these other two men got to do, assisting their leader directly from a much more secure, more prestigious position. In fact, credit for this amazing victory in the end would be ascribed to Aaron and Hur, who held up Moses' heavy hands when the battle started going against Israel, not to Joshua's keen planning and fearless courage. While Joshua was down in the trenches getting his hands dirty in the battle, the others were perched high up on the hill assisting their leader in prayer.

Have you ever felt as though God's task for you was beneath your capabilities or at least not as spiritual or successful or noticeable as someone else's? Has it ever seemed that others are always getting the credit for the work you're doing behind the scenes? While you watch others lead worship, teach Bible studies, or serve in ways that attract attention and earn them props, you find yourself laboring in the trenches, doing far less glamorous tasks. Changing diapers, working a corporate job, helping an elderly person shop for groceries—these seem fairly meaningless compared to what the "spiritual people" are getting to do.

This is such a common feeling. My friend Tara wishes so badly to be in full-time ministry, but so far the only positions she can find in Christian work are administrative in nature, not at all what she feels most qualified and hungry for.

Bernadette has three siblings but they all live out of state. She has become the primary caregiver for their aging parents.

Laura signed up to be a volunteer for the women's conference at her church. She just received her assignment in today's mail: bathroom duty.

Angela has led a women's Bible study for twelve years. She thought by now she'd be teaching larger groups, but she still only has a steady attendance of about twenty-five.

Leigh is a single mom who can barely find time to think straight, much less make time for doing any more at church or involving herself in ministry projects.

You may feel like adding your name to this list of people who wish for more but don't see it happening in their present context. But are you willing—as Joshua was—to take the post assigned to you for this moment in time? I'm not talking about the one you may be tapped for at a later season of life but the one God is making available to you right now. Since Promised Land living is largely about knowing, accepting, and doing God's will for us, we must heed Joshua's example and do our assigned task with our whole hearts. He was willing to stay in his lane, fulfilling the role to which God had appointed him.

How might this kind of lifestyle adjustment affect what you do in the next week or so? Abundant living is often that close to those who are willing to do well what's right in front of them.

## 3. Adopt a Willingness to Stand Alone

Moving ahead on Joshua's time line, we come to Numbers 13, the famous account of the twelve spies who were sent in by Moses to investigate the flora and fauna and potential fears of Canaan. We looked at this a few chapters ago in light of the men who came back trembling in the knees at what conquest would cost. This was the oasis-sitting lifestyle, the wilderness-wandering lifestyle that keeps people outside the Promised Land, always just a bit east of where God's abundance is waiting to be experienced.

Only Caleb and Joshua came back saying, "We should by all means go up and take possession of it, for we will surely overcome it" (v. 30). As someone has observed, "The ten saw God, if at all, only through the difficulties of the situation. These two men saw the difficulties through God. In one case the difficulties minimized God. In the other God minimized the difficulties."[18] Yet still theirs was a minority report so unpopular that the "whole community threatened to stone them" if not for the glory of the Lord appearing and putting everyone in their place (Num. 14:10 HCSB).

Let me tell you, being one-in-a-million is pretty much a guarantee that you'll have to stand alone at times. Taking God at His Word is rarely a popular position. When these two men with the "different spirit" stood two against two million, refusing to back down from their confident stance that God was more than able to make this milk-and-honey land their own, the backlash was loud, long, and uncomfortable. But no way did that sway their resolve. They stuck to their faith guns even when others were wanting to blast these guys away with them.

Several years ago God first began to speak to me about the inheritance He had in store for me in my spiritual life. As I asked more questions and got more answers, it became apparent that I would have to make some tough decisions about whether or not I was willing to go where God was asking me to go, even if others would not. There were certain believers I'd known for a long time who didn't approve of what I was considering. My search for an abundant relationship with God through His Spirit was taking me into uncharted territory that many would not traverse.

What's a good Christian girl to do? Would I stay spiritually complacent, apathetic to God's voice, or would I put my full trust in Him—not only trusting Him to take care of my journey but also to take care of my relationships as well?

I may still be a long way from being totally Joshua-like, but I know how it feels to stand in the minority, with God's call tugging you one direction and many well-meaning friends tugging you the other. We're not here to win popularity contests; we're here to conquer Canaan. A lot of women who win Miss Wilderness pageants don't realize they've settled for a crown that's not worth having. One-in-a-millions are after a much bigger prize. And they realize they may have to forgo popularity to get it.

## 4. Act Immediately

When the book closed on Moses' reign as leader, it didn't take long for Joshua to realize that he had not just been given a promotion to a new position. He had been called by God to take Canaan, to claim the land of promise. In Joshua 2, when he sent a new set of spies across the border into Jericho—the ones who ended up at Rahab's house—his reasons were much different from what his predecessors's had been. This mission wasn't designed as a way to put a moist finger in the wind but only to plot their initial attack point for beginning the conquest. Little surprise that as soon as these undercover agents returned, Joshua prepared to lead the people out on mission.

And please don't miss when he did it. "Then Joshua rose early in the morning" (Josh. 3:1). Obedience was his top priority. First thing on his list for the day. He acted *immediately* in response to God's direction.

I love the fact that the Scriptures are replete with the marvelous activity of God that occurred "early in the morning." When

Abraham obeyed God's unthinkable request to take his son, the child of promise, up to Mount Moriah and sacrifice him to the Lord there, he immediately obeyed. He left out from home with Isaac "early in the morning" (Gen. 22:3) to do what God had shown him.

During the Hebrews' ordeal in Egypt, God instructed Moses to "rise early in the morning" and present himself before Pharaoh (Exod. 8:20), telling the pagan ruler to let these people go.

When David left home for what would become his epic battle with Goliath of Gath, he "arose early in the morning" (1 Sam. 17:20) to meet up with Israel's army.

The women who initially discovered that Jesus had risen from the dead were able to be the first witnesses of His resurrection because they had come to the tomb "early in the morning" (Luke 24:22).

More than once in the book of Joshua, we see Israel's new leader rising up early, mustering the people, rousing his sleeping countrymen with an appeal to take courage and take action. This is more than just a foreshadowing of how important it is to meet God early in our twenty-four-hour day. It is a call for us to make obedience to His Word a priority on our to-do list and in every decision-making process. It's a reminder not to procrastinate when God is calling but rather to obey first and let everything else take care of itself.

I don't know what God is asking you to do right now—a change He's telling you to make, a bold ministry idea He's been stirring in your heart. But I know that if God is calling you to do it, He's not sitting around waiting to hear all your excuses for putting this off, all your reasons for why you think He's expecting too much of you here, why next month or next year would be much more convenient.

What is God asking you to do? Are you doing it?

Start. Today.

## 5. Activate Your Faith

When the children of Israel stood at the Jordan River—their final barrier to reaching Canaan—it was April. It was harvest season. Mount Hermon to the north was melting most of its winter snow and draining its runoff into the lower elevations. This had turned the once-calm Jordan into a raging body of water, as much as fifty times wider than at other times of the year. Today the Jordan looks like a placid and calm respite because of the modern dams that have been built. But on the day Israel crossed, it was more like the Colorado River at flood stage. If they thought God should have checked Google Earth before starting the journey to Canaan, they most assuredly thought He should have checked His calendar before leading them to the Jordan. This didn't seem like the best time of year to be planning a river crossing.

And for "three days" (Josh. 3:2), the children of Israel sat and stared at this. They could see it, hear it, feel it, taste it. They had three days to let the reality of this humongous, ultimate, giant-sized challenge wash over them as they considered how God would accomplish the first step: getting two million people across this watery death trap.

They'd heard about what happened at the Red Sea. Always sounded like such an amazing story. Always wished they'd been there. But now it was *their* feet at the water's edge. It was *their* faith being told to believe the impossible. These were deep, raging waters they were looking at, and the thought of trying to get across them alive was scaring them to death.

I'm sure you've stood on the seashore of your life and wondered how in the world you were supposed to get to the other side. You may be standing there right this minute, growing more afraid with each passing day, squinting across at where you need to go, shaking in your boots at the thought of what it's going to take.

But the deeper the waters, the greater the opportunity to see the supernatural power of God. The more angry the rapids, the bigger the celebration when He performs a miracle that helps you accomplish the unimaginable. When you're up against the enormity of an impossible challenge, it means God is up to something even more incredible than you can imagine, and He's asking you to move ahead in faith even when it seems impossible.

More than thirty years ago, my father pastored our church of around a hundred members. There was barely enough money in the budget and the offering plate to cover the cost of current expenses, much less anything extra. But Dad had become convinced that God was calling the church to a particular strip of land, the ideal site for our future sanctuary and campus.

One day, in a physical demonstration of his faith in God's testimony to him, my father put on his tennis shoes and walked up and down the road that he felt God would give them. He talked to the Lord with each step, making sure to plant his feet on every part of the property he believed God had promised.

Today, Oak Cliff Bible Fellowship Church ministers to our community from these same sixty-six acres of land my father walked on decades ago. Not only does a beautiful sanctuary and educational complex stand there but also a youth center, an elementary and middle school, a community outreach center, and a pregnancy care center—all because one man heard God, believed Him, and then boldly walked into the place God had promised.

I think we can safely conclude that Joshua didn't know exactly how he was going to get two million Israelites across a swollen river and into the land God had told him to inhabit and conquer, any more than my dad knew exactly how he was going to lead our church to the property God had led him to. But Joshua took God at His word. He packed up the gear and pulled these people seven miles from Shittim to the edge of the Jordan River. He was going in. God had said it. So he planned to do it.

It's important to bear in mind that Joshua was acting on a clear word from the Lord. Yahweh had given him clear instructions: "Arise, cross this Jordan, you and all this people, to the land which I am giving to them" (Josh. 1:2). The kind of faith he exercised in moving forward despite seemingly insurmountable odds was founded on a sure Word from the Lord. In fact, his confidence to do so was based on His certainty in God's instructions to him. We must practice discerning the voice of God so that we're only acting on things He's really saying. Nothing is much more exhausting and discouraging than waving our spiritual courage around based on our own best guesses. You and I can't just decide what we want God to do, choose to act on it, then get frustrated when He doesn't respond. We must wait to hear Him, stay faithful to the principles of Scripture, and then follow His leading. This is what it means to walk by the Spirit.

And this is the Joshua paradigm for all of us who want to be the one-in-a-million that crosses over into Promised Land living. He saw the same swirling waters everyone else did on that early morning at Gilgal (the point at which Israel crossed the Jordan). But having heard God's command to move forward, he refused to let even an outrageous obstacle like this deter him. With nothing but God's Word that told him this raging Jordan River had a means of being crossed by two million people, He put all his trust in God. Don't expect to enter into abundance without having to call on that kind of faith.

## 6. Acknowledge God's Presence

My husband has one of those GPS systems in his car to help him figure out how to get wherever he needs to go. He can just pop in the address of his desired destination, and this little unit is designed to calculate a set of turn-by-turn directions. Now maybe I'm a little old-school here, but I still prefer calling people on the phone who either live or work at the place I'm trying to reach and just letting them tell me the best, quickest, most convenient way to get there. Surely they know more than any little machine can. But that's not the way my man rolls. And usually, thankfully, his little gadget does the trick.

Usually.

I remember flying into Mississippi with him one day for a speaking engagement. We didn't know exactly how to find the church that had scheduled us to be there, but Jerry had brought along his GPS locator. And as if that wasn't enough, the rental car we picked up at the airport had one as well. So to be on the safe side—or perhaps just as a natural reaction to having this much raw technology at his fingertips—he programmed both GPS systems to compare their conclusions. (Please.)

Three hours later neither unit had been able to get us to Point B or anywhere near. It was only the restraining power of the Holy Spirit keeping me in my seat. I was thinking if my husband didn't pick up that other technological marvel real soon, his cell phone, I was going to do physical harm to something or to somebody.

When he finally consented to calling our contact person at the church, I could hear her sympathetic voice coming loud and clear through the receiver, saying, "Oh, I wish you'd have called me sooner." (You and me both.) "Back here where we are, we have some new roads that aren't even paved. The GPS systems haven't picked up on them yet. We're the only ones who know where they are."

What is it with men and directions? Some have suggested, humorously and yet somewhat rightly so, that the reason the Israelites wandered for so long in the wilderness was because Moses was too stubborn to ask for some.

But not Joshua.

He knew that forty years was long enough for anyone to be lost. And now that he was in the driver's seat, he decided they were going to do what they should have done in the first place—put their confidence in Someone who had already been here and walked this road.

Rather than continue to trust their own devices, Joshua was ready to acknowledge that God's directions were far more reliable than man's were. He wisely told the people why—"for you have not passed this way before" (Josh. 3:4). May as well stop wasting time and follow Someone who knows their way around these parts. "As for me and my house" (Josh. 24:15), Joshua was following his Lord.

Here's what he told his officers to say to the people as they stood at the water's edge: "When you see the ark of the covenant of the Lord your God with the Levitical priests carrying it, then you shall set out from your place and go after it" (Josh. 3:3). This was such an important principle to Joshua that the ark of the covenant (the representation of God's presence) is mentioned as many as ten times in this third chapter alone. In other words, wherever God goes, that's where you are to go. But if God doesn't go, then we aren't going. Joshua didn't say, "I'm the leader. Follow me." He said, "God's the leader. Follow Him."

If you and I are going to cross over and live in the abundance Christ died for us to possess, we must keep our eyes peeled for God's presence and activity and then follow hard after Him. We must ask Him to heighten our awareness of Him, sharpening our spiritual sensitivity so that just as our five physical senses pick up on sights and sounds in the natural realm, our spiritual senses can pick up on God's movement in the spiritual realm. God is moving, and when we recognize His activity around us, it's an invitation for us to get on board with what He is doing.

This is what Jesus did while He was in ministry on Earth. Wonder how many good things He turned away from in order to "do only what He [saw] his Father doing"? (John 5:19 NIV). Jesus knew what you and I must learn: not every good thing is a God thing, and *nothing* is worth doing if it's not what God wants us to do. What astounds me about Jesus' life on Earth is that He not only did the Father's will; He did the Father's will . . . and nothing else!

Can I be honest? I'm interested in doing God's will, but I am often too tired to get around to it because I've been preoccupied with other good things. You too? When we get busy doing everything else along the way, our energy is zapped—physically, emotionally, mentally, and spiritually. So by the time we finally get around to doing what God is leading us to do, we're so exhausted from all the other stuff, we're low on energy to fulfill the very thing we were supposed to be focused on.

Joshua was finished with caving to fear, going in circles, and chasing distractions. He was tired of working hard every day and finding himself no closer to Canaan. It was time to go where God was leading. And nowhere else. Enough was enough. No more side jobs. No more deterrents. No more time-wasters. He was looking for God and following Him and Him alone.

He was that kind of leader. We must be that kind of people.


## 7. Anticipate God's Miracles

Joshua was serious about obeying immediately and was a confident, fearless leader. He accepted His job assignment without excuse or frustration and looked for God's presence as his only marching orders. But not only that, he was a man who anticipated God's miracles, fully expecting the unexpected. As he drew the people up close to where the Jordan was raging against its own banks, it would have made sense for him to say, "Sharpen your swords" or "Prepare your shields," but instead he told them, "Consecrate yourselves, for tomorrow the LORD will do wonders among you" (Josh. 3:5).

Aah, "wonders"—a word the New International Version translates as "amazing things."

In essence he was instructing the people of Israel to start acting like they knew God was going to do something incredible. He told them to consecrate, purify, and set themselves apart *today* in anticipation of the miracle that God would perform *tomorrow*. It's one thing to change the way you're living *after* God parts the Jordan. It's another to do it while the waves of your problem are still crashing around your feet as you stand on the shore.

It takes faith to look at a problem and begin living as though God is going to do something spectacular in the midst of it. It takes faith, knowing your personal, family, or community situation the way you do, to start walking in patient confidence that God hasn't conceded defeat in your life. It takes faith to look at an obstacle that is deeper and meaner than any courage you can conjure up yet be absolutely assured that God's power is more than enough to move it out of the way.

The woman who founded my college sorority was a person who demonstrated this principle to me, leaving an indelible imprint. I recall a time when she was in the midst of a deep financial struggle but was trusting God to increase her income at work. After much prayer, after an intense time of listening for His direction, she felt confident that God would answer her request. So she began tithing from the amount she was expecting to receive—before the money was actually in her hand to give! She knew her miracle was coming.

As a college sophomore, I was amazed at her boldness of belief. I mean, what kind of obedient heart gives money to the Lord that He hasn't even supplied yet, already confident that He is going to do it? But God saw her heart, knew her willingness to follow Him, and opened her ears to hear a sure word from Him regarding her finances. She then acted in faith *before* seeing God move.

I encourage you today to start acting as though God is already up to big things. Wonderful things. "Amazing things." Instead of waiting to respond at a later, more convenient time, go ahead and begin your preboarding. "Consecrate" yourself by packing all your passions into a pure obedience toward God and His Word. And see how Canaan feels when God enables you to sink your sandals down into it.

Massive giants and minority reports had been the Israelites' old method of dealing with difficulties. The Moses method. It had kept them alive but at the unbearable expense of living outside the boundaries of Promised Land experience. Joshua had now brought them a new paradigm.

1. Advance with courage.
2. Accept your post.
3. Adopt a willingness to stand alone.
4. Act immediately.
5. Activate your faith.
6. Acknowledge God's presence.
7. Anticipate God's miracles.

And within a matter of hours, their first set of footprints would be pressed into Promised Land soil—even if it took a Red Sea miracle in the middle of the Jordan River to do it.

## Crossing Over

Joshua gave the word, the one he had heard from the Lord, the one that made this forty-year odyssey seem as though it were finally going to end in triumph. It was finally going to take them where they'd been headed all this time. After decades of roundabout wandering, the children of Israel were about to walk a miraculous straight line into the Promised Land.

The people woke up on that expectant morning, brought their entire families out of their tents, and approached the swirling rapids of the Jordan. The priests who carried the ark of God stepped off the bank into the shallow east edge of the water.

At first it would have appeared as if nothing was happening since the water didn't immediately divide right in front of them. But what the children of Israel didn't know as they craned their necks to the north was that far upstream God was already working His miracle for them. Though the roar of the current continued to drown out conversations, clearly mitigating against a mass river crossing, "the waters which were flowing down from above stood and rose up in one heap, a great distance away at Adam, the city that is beside Zarethan" (Josh. 3:16). Adam was thirty miles away. At this place, far out of sight, the Jordan was even then starting to become a dry riverbed. It was going to take a little while for the runoff to spill through at the Israelites' downstream location, but the miracle was already in progress.[19]

From your current vantage point you may not be able to see how God is going to work out His purposes in your life, the ones that seem far away and impossible to detect. You've gotten your feet wet, but life just seems to roll on like it always has, oblivious to your prayers and the faith you've placed in God's clear word to you. But be convinced that eventhough God may be working "a great distance" away, He is working. He has not forgotten His promises. He has not run into a snag that may prevent Him from following through. As you faithfully incorporate the new paradigm of Joshua's leadership into your life, be assured that God will carry out the miraculous plans He has for you. And you will see them with your own eyes, just as the Hebrews did when the remaining waves, stripped of their energy source, emptied out before them like water down a storm drain.

> Those which were flowing down toward the sea of the Arabah, the Salt Sea, were completely cut off. So the people crossed opposite Jericho. And the priests who carried the ark of the covenant of the LORD stood firm on dry ground in the middle of the Jordan while all Israel crossed on dry ground, until all the nation had finished crossing the Jordan. (Josh. 3:16–17)

"All the nation."
Across.
They made it.
And so can we.

# A Final Thought

ROGER BANNISTER WAS A BRITISH distance runner who dreamed of running a four-minute mile. It was a feat deemed impossible by nearly everyone in the sport and certainly by the average spectator in the crowd and on the street. No one could do it, not even the fastest men in the world. But after coming up short on numerous occasions, failing even to medal in the 1952 Olympics, Roger's drive and determination paid off on May 6, 1954, when he became the first man on Earth to record a four-minute mile in actual competition. The impossible barrier had fallen. There was one person who could do it.

But within little more than a month, another miler had done it. Within a year, thirty had done it. Today the world record for the mile stands at nearly seventeen seconds faster. Nearly *everyone* who races competitively at major levels can run a four-minute mile.

It just took someone—a one-in-a-million—to break through the barrier first. And now the barriers are falling every day.

Do you remember where this book started—with me as a ten-year-old girl, observing someone from my seat on the church pew who was already living in Canaan and had the testimony to prove it? What starts with one—what starts with you—can change a life, can change a generation, can change who knows how many others by the Promised Land experience you live, just as that woman's changed mine. You can help lead untold numbers to discover their true destiny in Christ.

You may be the only person in your family who's ever broken the barrier, the only one brave enough to stop doing what everyone else has been doing. You may be the only one in your circle of friends who's willing to break the cultural code and believe what others only sit around talking about. You may even be one of the few in your *church* who are tired of playing wilderness games, who have had a bellyful of boring oasis life and are after a little milk and honey instead. You may be required to stand alone for a while. You may look kind of foolish following that ark into the impossible, impassable waters of your personal situation, praising God in the face of life's steady resistance to spiritual realities. But when God carries you through to the other side—and He will, my friend, He will—you probably won't be left standing in Canaan all by yourself. Others will want to follow a God who can do what He does in people like you.

Yes, when Joshua and Caleb stepped up out of the Jordan riverbed and looked off into Canaan, they weren't there by themselves. There were millions more circling up behind them, inspired by their fearless faith in God to seek a Promised Land lifestyle for themselves. One-in-a-millions don't live this way because they love being loners and mavericks. They do it to be faithful. And in so doing, in breaking down the barriers, they blaze one contagious trail to glory.

I hope this isn't the last time we get to be together like this. But I have enough confidence in God's Word and His Spirit to know that He will lead each of us faithfully, even while we're apart—delivering us, developing us, enabling us to break through the barriers to experience our destiny, helping us make a real difference in the places where we live.

Let's promise to be praying for one another that we can continue to be the barrier breakers. Let's seek out the people who can help us be all God wants us to be. Let's want nothing more in life than to experience Him, to hear His voice, and to be part of the supernatural work He is doing in our midst, in our day.

From the pew to the pavement. From the slave pit to Sinai. From the oasis of complacency to the land of promise.

I'm going.

Let's go there together.

# APPENDIX

# Promised Land Living

THESE ARE SOME OF THE things that characterize the life of someone who is experiencing the abundant life offered by Christ. While perfection in these areas will not be achieved while we are on Earth, they can and should be the overarching experience of the believer. Remember, the Israelites faced enemies as soon as they crossed the Jordan, so Promised Land living does not mean a life with no problems. It is a life that experiences God's power and presence in spite of difficulty. You know you are living in the land of abundance not when your circumstances change but when this list describes your life—even when circumstances have not changed.

- Sensing the indwelling of the Holy Spirit (*Ephesians 1:13–14; Romans 8:9*)
- Being led by the Spirit of God (*Romans 8:14*)
- Being able to recognize and tear down strongholds (*2 Corinthians 10:4*)
- Valuing spiritual abundance over physical (*Luke 12:15*)
- Being free from a lifestyle of sin (*Galatians 5:1; Romans 6:18; 1 Peter 2:24*)
- Showing evidence of conformity to Christ's image (*Romans 8:29*)

- Having confidence in a standing of righteousness before the Father (*Philippians 3:9; Romans 10:4; 2 Corinthians 5:21*)
- Having confidence in eternal life (*Titus 1:2*)
- Continually casting anxiety and worry on God (*1 Peter 5:7; Philippians 4:6*)
- Able to give thanks in spite of difficult circumstances (*Philippians 4:6*)
- Rejoices to share in Christ's sufferings (*1 Peter 4:13; Hebrews 10:32–35*)
- Can endure trials (*1 Corinthians 10:13*)
- Sensing God's comfort and hope (*2 Thessalonians 2:16; 2 Corinthians 1:3–5*)
- Having confidence to draw near to God (*Hebrews 7:25; Hebrews 10:19*)
- Living as an alien and stranger to this world (*1 Peter 2:11*)
- Is able to hear the voice of God (*John 10:27*)
- Is able to discern the guidance of the Holy Spirit (*John 16:13*)
- Believing that God is the source to supply their every need (*Philippians 4:19*)
- Is open to receiving the gifts given by the Holy Spirit (*1 Corinthians 12:4–7*)
- Recognizing and utilizing spiritual gifts for the edification of Christ's body (*1 Peter 4:10; 1 Corinthians 4:7*)
- Displaying the fruit of the Holy Spirit in daily living (*Galatians 5:22; Psalm 92:12–14; John 15:5*)
- Experiencing an overwhelming and constant sense of joy (*John 15:11; Psalm 16:11*)
- Experiencing an overwhelming and constant sense of peace (*Philippians 4:7*)
- Recognizing and utilizing the spiritual armor available for spiritual battle (*Ephesians 6:10–18*)

- Desiring to know and do God's predetermined will (*Ephesians 2:10; Psalm 40:8; Psalm 119:33*)
- Expecting that God is able to do more than they can ask or think (*Ephesians 3:20; 1 Corinthians 2:9*)
- Believing God's promises regardless of circumstances (*Genesis 15:6; Genesis 22:6–14*)
- Appropriating God's Promises (*Romans 4:21; 2 Corinthians 7:1; James 1:22*)
- Willingly accepting and excelling at whatever God has called you to do (*Exodus 17:8–13*)
- Speaking boldly about the goodness of God (*Psalm 145:6; Acts 3:1–10; Acts 4:7–12*)
- Speaking boldly about the gospel of Jesus Christ (*Romans 1:16*)
- Living to please the Lord (*2 Corinthians 5:9; 1 Thessalonians 2:4; Hebrews 13:21*)
- Expecting to see the miracles of God (*Galatians 3:5*)
- Fully anticipating to experience God's power (*1 Chronicles 29:12*)
- Sensing and acknowledging God's continual presence with them (*Psalms 139:7–10*)
- Is content with what they have (*Philippians 4:12; Hebrews 13:5*)
- Encouraging others to live a godly life (*Hebrews 10:24*)
- Confesses sin and believes they are forgiven (*1 John 1:9*)
- Committing to obeying God's commands (*Psalm 1:2; John 14:21*)
- Values connection with the body of Christ (*Acts 2:46; Hebrews 10:25*)
- Pursuing unity in the body of Christ (*Ephesians 4:2–6; Romans 14:19*)

- Displaying divine power in weakness (*1 Corinthians 2:3–5; 2 Corinthians 12:10*)
- Forgiving when wronged (*Matthew 18:21–22; Colossians 3:13*)
- Living in anticipation of the return of Christ (*Philippians 3:20*)
- Continuing to pursue the things of God throughout life (*Genesis 5:23–24; Psalm 119:33*)

# Notes

† If you are not sure you've ever given your heart to Christ and been forgiven of your sins, delivered from spiritual bondage, I urge you to let this be the day that you surrender it all to Him. He has already done the hard work—dying to pay the price for your sins on the cross (Rom. 5:6–9), then rising again to conquer the final enemy of death on your behalf (1 Cor. 15:20–22). All that's left is for you to realize that you're a sinner, desperately in need of being rescued (Rom. 3:23–24), and to believe that Jesus is your only hope for salvation (Acts 4:11). This is only the beginning point of your life together with Him, but it is absolutely essential before you can expect to move one step forward. It'll never be you doing great things for God; it'll be God doing great things through you, a man or woman made holy by Christ's sacrifice and made capable of experiencing Him (1 John 3:1–3).

1. Francis Brown, Samuel Rolles Driver, and Charles Briggs, *Enhanced Brown-Driver-Briggs Hebrew and English Lexicon*, electronic edition (Oak Habor, WA: Logos Research Systems, 2000), xiii.

2. Quoted in *Exodus: Saved for God's Glory*, Philip Graham Ryken (Wheaton, IL: Crossway, 2005), 153.

3. Iain M. Duguid, *Numbers: God's Presence in the Wilderness* (Wheaton, IL: Crossway, 2006), 150.

4. Ibid., 148.

5. Tommy Tenney, *The God Catchers Workbook: Experiencing the Manifest Presence of God* (Nashville, TN: Thomas Nelson, 2008), 56.

6. William Lee Holliday, ed., *A Concise Hebrew and Aramaic Lexicon of the Old Testament* (Grand Rapids, MI: Eerdmans, 1972), 234. Accessed through Logos Bible Software.

7. Ryken, *Exodus*, 380.

8. H. D. M. Spence, Joseph S. Exell, eds., *The Pulpit Commentary* (Peabody, MA: Hendrickson, 1985).

9. Ryken, *Exodus*, 419.

10. John D. Currid, *Ancient Egypt and the Old Testament* (Grand Rapids, MI: Baker Academic, 1997), 145.

11. Ryken, *Exodus*, 416.

12. Albert Lindsey, *Wilderness Experiences: Practical Studies from the Book of Exodus* (Grand Rapids, MI: Zondervan, 1942), 51.

13. *New American Standard Hebrew-Aramaic and Greek Dictionaries*, Logos, #3513.

14. Ryken, *Exodus*, 493.

15. Harold L. Willmington, *Willmington Book of Bible Lists* (Carol Stream, IL: Tyndale House Publishers, 1987).

16. Sam Pascoe quote, see http://www.geocitites.com/raqta24/Christ.htm.

17. John F. Walvoord, Roy B. Zuck. *The Bible Knowledge Commentary* (Wheaton, IL: Victor Books, 1985), 1:328.

18. James Hastings, *Greater Men and Women of the Bible* (New York, NY: C. Scribner's Sons), 370.

19. A Commentary and Critical and Explanatory on the Old and New Testament, Joshua 3:16, Logos Bible Software.

**My Promised Land:** *To laugh like I used to.*

*one* in a million

Priscilla Shirer

As God's child, I know He has freed me. I know He is with me. I know He has given me precious promises. But sometimes I don't live like I believe it.

Join Priscilla for a Bible study that will challenge you to conquer your wilderness living and learn what it means to live free in Jesus Christ. This is your one-in-a-million opportunity to fully engage in the abundant inheritance God has waiting for those who are willing to follow Him into the promised land.

*Experience your deliverance.*
*Conquer your wilderness.*
*Claim your inheritance.*

See Priscilla Shirer live at
**Deeper Still** and **Going Beyond** events.

www.lifeway.com/**women**
800.458.2772 • LifeWay Christian Stores

**LifeWay** | **Women**

LIFEWAY WOMEN *events*

# LET HIM TAKE YOU BEYOND

## Going**BEYOND**

is an intimate and inspiring women's conference like no other. Come spend time with passionate Bible teacher **Priscilla Shirer** as she encourages you from God's Word and leads you in an unforgettable prayer experience. Enjoy special worship led by **Anthony Evans**.

For tickets, dates or more information call 800.254.2022 or visit lifeway.com/goingbeyond

REGISTER TODAY!

Locations and dates subject to change without notice.

LifeWay | Wom